GW01091199

AVIATION FIRSTS
336 Questions and Answers

Joshua Stoff

DOVER PUBLICATIONS, INC.
Mineola, New York

Copyright

Copyright © 2000 by Dover Publications, Inc.
All rights reserved under Pan American and International Copyright Conventions.

Published in Canada by General Publishing Company, Ltd., 30 Lesmill Road, Don Mills, Toronto, Ontario.

Bibliographical Note

Aviation Firsts: 336 Questions and Answers is a new work, first published by Dover Publications, Inc., in 2000.

Library of Congress Cataloging-in-Publication Data

Stoff, Joshua.
    Aviation firsts : 336 questions and answers / Joshua Stoff.
      p. cm.
    ISBN 0-486-41245-8 (pbk.)
    1. Aeronautics—Records—Miscellanea. I. Title.

TL537 .S76 2000
629.13'.09—dc21

                         00-060164

Manufactured in the United States of America
Dover Publications, Inc., 31 East 2nd Street, Mineola, N.Y. 11501

Introduction

Humans have probably longed to fly ever since man first began to reflect on the world around him. Studying the seemingly effortless flight of birds inspired dreamers to imagine a variety of methods for copying them. Although humankind's efforts to fly began thousands of years ago, future historians may well label the 20th century as the era of the development of manned flight, from the first hops at Kitty Hawk in 1903 to the supersonic aircraft and spacecraft of today.

More than two centuries of flight by man has seen many great moments in aviation, some wonderful, others tragic. During those centuries, thousands of feats have been performed by brave men and women in everything from balloons to spacecraft. It took countless years, and many heartbreaking efforts before man could take to the sky with ease. Aviation history is full of stories of courage, daring, and determination. Little progress could have been made without that special breed of men and women willing to risk their reputation and lives for its advance.

This book offers a compilation of many of the fascinating highlights of man's efforts to conquer the sky and the heavens. It provides a simple running history of the development of aviation and spaceflight. It is hoped that this chronology will provide a valuable tool for a wide variety of people. People often wonder who, what, or when about aviation, and this work seeks to establish reliable dates for events in the aerospace field. It is surprising how wide the field is from which inquiries come— from aerospace executives, to journalists, to students, to barroom patrons in heated argument. Perhaps many of these questions can now be answered quickly and easily.

18th and 19th Centuries

1. Who was the first human being to fly? The first person to fly, in a hot air balloon, was François Pilâtre de Rozier of France, who on October 15, 1783, rose to a height of 84 feet on a tether. The hot air was provided by a straw fire below the balloon. On November 21, 1783, de Rozier and Marquis d'Arlandes made the world's first free flight when their balloon flew 5½ miles across Paris. They reached a maximum altitude of about 1000 feet in the 50-foot diameter Montgolfier balloon.

2. Who was the first woman to fly? The first woman to fly, in a hot air balloon, was the Countess de Montalembert, who made a tethered flight in a Montgolfier hot air balloon on May 20, 1784, in Paris.

3. Who was the first person to be killed in a balloon? The first person to be killed while ballooning was Pilâtre de Rozier on June 15, 1785. De Rozier was attempting to fly across the English Channel when his combination hot air and hydrogen balloon caught fire and crashed. The balloon crashed near Boulogne, also killing de Rozier's companion, Jules Romain.

4. Who made the first balloon flight in America? The first flight by a balloon in the United States was made on January 9, 1793, by the Frenchman Jean Pierre Blanchard. Blanchard rose in a hydrogen balloon from Philadelphia and landed in Gloucester, New Jersey, 46 minutes later.

5. Who was the first American aeronaut? The first American to fly in America was New Yorker Charles Durant. On September 9, 1830, he ascended from Castle Garden, New York, in his balloon, landing in South Amboy, New Jersey two hours later.

6. When was a balloon first used in warfare? The first military reconnaissance by a balloon was made by J. M. Coutelle for the French army at the Battle of Maubeuge on June 2, 1794. The balloon *Entreprenant* was also used for observations against the Austrians at the Battle of Fleurus on June 26, 1794.

7. When was the balloon first used for military purposes in America? The balloon was first used by the American military on October 1, 1861,

1

during the Civil War, when the Federal Balloon Corps was formed with five balloons and fifty men under the command of Thaddeus Lowe. They were first used in combat on May 31, 1862 when a Union tethered balloon, piloted by T. S. Lowe, saved Union forces from defeat at the Battle of Fair Oaks, Virginia.

8. What was the first long-distance international balloon flight? The first long-distance international balloon flight was made by Charles Green of England in a gas balloon. In July 1836 he flew from London to Nassau, Germany—480 miles in 18 hours.

9. Who was the first person to make a parachute jump? The first ever parachute descent was made by the Frenchman André Garnerin, who jumped from a balloon at 3000 feet near Paris, on October 22, 1797.

10. Who made the first parachute jump in America? The first parachute descent from a balloon in America was made by Charles Guille on August 2, 1819. Guille jumped from a hydrogen balloon at 8000 feet over Brooklyn, New York.

11. Who was the first person to be carried aloft in a heavier-than-air craft? In 1853 an unknown ten-year-old boy became airborne in a glider constructed by Sir George Cayley near Scarborough, Yorkshire, England. The boy, son of one of Cayley's estate workers, became airborne in the glider after it was towed downhill by manpower into a breeze.

12. Who was the first person to fly a powered heavier-than-air craft (unmanned)? American professor Samuel P. Langley of the Smithsonian Institution became interested in aeronautics in the 1880s, and, in the 1890s built powered aircraft with 14-foot wingspans. With the help of Augustus Herring, Langley developed a tandem-monoplane steam-powered aircraft that first flew successfully when catapulted from a houseboat on the Potomac River in May, 1896. Langley's longest flights with this aircraft, *Aerodrome #5,* measured over ¾ mile and included controlled turns and stable climbing flight. This aircraft was built as a precursor to a full-sized, man-carrying aircraft, which failed miserably when launched in 1903.

13. When was the world's first powered airship built? The world's first powered, manned dirigible flew on September 24, 1852, when the Frenchman Henri Giffard flew his 144-foot long, steam-engine powered non-rigid airship from the Paris Hippodrome. The 17-mile flight to Trappes was made at an average speed of 5 mph. This flight was only tentative, but it marked the beginning of the practical airship.

14. What was the world's first successful rigid airship? The first flight in a rigid airship was made by Count Ferdinand Von Zeppelin's LZ-1 on July 2, 1900. The 420-foot long, aluminum-framed airship carried five people on a 20-minute flight over Germany's Lake Constance, at a speed of 9 mph.

15. Who was the first person to attempt a flight across the Atlantic Ocean? On October 6, 1873, Washington H. Donaldson attempted the first flight across the Atlantic Ocean, in a gas balloon. Financed by the *New York Daily Illustrated Graphic,* the 600,000-cubic-foot balloon lifted off from the Capitoline Grounds, Brooklyn. Along with Donaldson was a navigator, Alfred Ford, and George Lunt, a reporter. After crossing Long Island and the Long Island Sound, the balloon ran into a severe thunderstorm over Connecticut and was forced down six hours later.

16. Who was the first person to make a controlled glider flight? The first person to make sustained, controlled gliding flights was Otto Lilienthal of Germany. Between 1891 and 1896, Lilienthal made over 2000 glides, some of them several hundred feet, down a large hill he had constructed near Berlin. His gliders were mostly monoplanes with fixed tails, and limited control was achieved by shifting the pilot's body weight. Unfortunately, Lilienthal was killed when one of his gliders was upset by a sudden gust of wind in 1896. Thus he also became the first person to be killed in an aircraft.

The Pioneers: 1902–1913

17. Who made the first powered flights in the United States? The first powered flights in the United States were made by Leo Stevens and Edward Boice in two small airships over Brooklyn, New York, on September 30, 1902. Stevens flew an airship of his own design, while Boice was flying the Santos-Dumont Number 6. Equipped with 10 horsepower gasoline engines, both airships made flights of about 45 minutes in front of thousands of spectators.

18. Who built the first successful man-carrying powered aircraft? The first heavier-than-air craft to achieve manned, powered, controlled flight was unquestionably the Wright Flyer of 1903. Built by Wilbur and Orville Wright of Dayton, Ohio, the Flyer evolved from several successful gliders built over a three-year period. In order to build a successful aircraft, the Wrights first had to develop a wing shape that would give them sufficient lift, a powerful gasoline engine, efficient propellers, and a revolutionary three-axis control system. The Wright Flyer first flew on December 17, 1903, at Kittyhawk, North Carolina. Four flights were made that first day, the longest covering about 852 feet in 59 seconds. When the Wrights finally gave public demonstration flights in 1908, they electrified the world and gave great impetus to the newborn aviation industry. Several others claim to have flown successfully prior to the Wrights' first flights, most notably Gustave Whitehead of Bridgeport, Connecticut in 1901. There is no documentary evidence to prove these claims, however.

19. Who was the first person killed in a powered aircraft? The first fatality of an airplane crash was Lieutenant Thomas Selfridge of the U.S. Army on September 17, 1908. The accident occurred at Fort Myer, Virginia, when a Wright biplane piloted by Orville Wright crashed, killing its passenger. The accident occurred during army acceptance trials of the new flying machine when a control wire broke or was cut by a propeller, causing the machine to crash from about 75 feet.

20. What was the world's first aircraft manufacturing company? The world's first aircraft manufacturing company was Voisin Frères, established in Billancourt, France in November 1906 by Gabriel and Charles

Voisin. The company originally had two employees. Their first order, received in December 1906, was for an ornithopter that never flew. Their first successful aircraft was a box kite-like biplane, built for Léon Delagrange, which flew in Bagatelle in March 1907.

21. Who built the world's first helicopter? The first helicopter to lift a man from the ground was built by the Bréguet brothers in France in 1907. Although this lifted a man from the ground on September 29 of that year, it was not free flight, as four men on the ground steadied the craft. However on November 13, 1907, a man-carrying helicopter built by Paul Cornu successfully flew near Lisieux, France. The twin-rotor free flying helicopter was powered by a 24-hp Antoinette engine.

22. What was the first official flight in Europe of at least one kilometer? The first official flight in Europe of at least one kilometer was made by Henri Farman on January 13, 1908. Flying a Voisin biplane, he flew just over one kilometer, in front of many witnesses, at Issy-les-Moulineaux.

23. Who made the first "cross-country" flight in an airplane? The first "cross-country" flight was made by Henri Farman on October 30, 1908. He flew from Bouy, France, to Rheims—14 miles in 20 minutes.

24. Who made the first flight in France? The first flight in France was made on November 12, 1906, by the Brazilian-born builder and pilot Alberto Santos-Dumont, in Paris. He flew his 14 bis 722 feet in 21 seconds. Basically the plane was a man-carrying box kite powered by a 50-hp Antoinette engine. This flight won him the French Aero Club's prize for the first flight of more than 100 meters.

25. Who made the first flight in Italy? The first flight in Italy was made by the French sculptor and aviator Léon Delagrange in Voisin in October 1907. Delagrange was killed flying a Blériot in 1910.

26. Who made the first flight in Germany? The first flight in Germany was made by the Dane, J. C. Ellehammer in a triplane of his own design at Kiel, in June 1907. A later version of this triplane was flown by the first German pilot, Hans Grade, at Magdeburg in October 1907.

27. Who made the first flight in Austria? The first flight in Austria was made by the Frenchman, G. Legagneaux at Vienna in April 1908 in a Voisin. The first Austrian to fly was Igo Etrich in a Taube in November 1908.

28. Who made the first flight in Russia? The first flight in Russia was made by V. Schkrouff in a Voisin at Odessa in July 1908.

29. Who made the first flight in Sweden? The first flight in Sweden was made by the Frenchman G. Legagneaux at Stockholm in his Voisin in July 1908.

30. Who made the first flight in Rumania? The first flight in Rumania was made by Louis Blériot in his monoplane at Bucharest in October 1908.

31. Who made the first flight in England? The first flight in England was made by the American Samuel F. Cody in his British Army Aeroplane No. 1 on October 16, 1908. The 1390-foot flight was made at Farnborough and ended in a crash landing.

32. Who made the first flight in Canada? The first flight in Canada was made by the Canadian J. A. D. McCurdy on February 23, 1909 over Baddeck Bay, Nova Scotia in the *Silver Dart.*

33. Who made the first flight in Ireland? The first flight in Ireland was made by H. G. Ferguson of Belfast in December 1909 in an airplane of his own design that resembled a Blériot.

34. Who made the first flight in Thailand (Siam)? The first flight in Thailand was made by Major Luang Sakdi Salyavudh of the Royal Siamese Army in December 1913 in a Nieuport.

35. Who made the first flight in Egypt? The first flight in Egypt was made by G. W. Dawes in a British-built Blériot at Heliopolis in January 1910.

36. Who made the first flight in Australia? The first flight in Australia was made by Colin Defries in an imported Wright biplane at Sydney in January 1910.

37. Who made the first flight in New Zealand? The first flight in New Zealand was made by the Frenchman Henri Pequet on February 18, 1911, in a Humber biplane, from Allahabad to Naini Junction—a distance of five miles.

38. Who was the first woman to fly in an airplane? The first woman to fly in an airplane was Frenchwoman Madame Thérèse Peltier, who was taken aloft by Léon Delagrange in a Voisin on July 8, 1908.

39. Who was the first pilot to be killed flying an airplane? The first pilot of a powered airplane to die while flying was Eugène Lefèbvre of France. He was killed while flying a Wright Model A in Port Juvisy, France on September 7, 1909.

40. Who was the first American woman to be killed in an airplane? The first American woman to be killed in a plane crash was Julie Clark of Denver, Colorado. On June 17, 1912, her Curtiss Model D struck a tree at Springfield, Illinois.

41. What was the world's first international air meet? The world's first international air meet was held in Rheims, France between August 22 and 29, 1909. Thirty-five aircraft competed for prizes for speed, altitude, endurance, and distance. Henri Farman of France established new records for duration and distance by flying 112 miles in 3 hours, 4 minutes. Glenn Curtiss took top honors for speed with a high of 45 mph.

42. What was the first international air meet in America? The first international air meet in America was at Belmont Park, Long Island, New York between October 22, and 31, 1910. Some 40 American and European aviators and aircraft participated, and crowds of 100,000 viewed the events daily. New altitude, endurance, and speed records were set. Perhaps the most exciting, and dangerous, race was from Belmont Park to the Statue of Liberty and back. The contest was won by American John Moisant in a very close, and disputed, finish over Englishman Claude Graham White.

43. What was America's first airport? Although there is some question as to what can be called an airport, or airfield (as opposed to just a place where one plane was test flown), America's first public flying field was most likely the one in Mineola, New York. Glenn Curtiss first brought his *Golden Flyer* there, in June, 1909, because he admired the flat, wide open spaces of Long Island's Hempstead Plains. By the end of July, the New York Aeronautic Society set up its headquarters there, and almost immediately there were a wide variety of airplanes on the field, either under construction, flying, or attempting to fly. Charles Willard took flying instructions from Glenn Curtiss in Mineola in July 1909, and by September, Henry Walden built his first successful monoplane on the field.

44. Who made the first public demonstration flights in an airplane in America? The first public demonstration of an airplane in America was made in Hammondsport, New York, on July 4, 1908. Glenn Curtiss, flying the *June Bug,* made a flight of over one mile in 1 minute 42 seconds, before a large crowd, to win the *Scientific American* trophy for the first flight of one kilometer.

45. Who was the first American to have a pilot's license? The first American to hold a pilot's license was Glenn Curtiss. On October 7, 1909, Curtiss was awarded an FAI *(Fédération Aéronautique Internationale)* certificate; he was given Aero Club of France Certificate #2.

46. Who was the first military pilot to solo? The first American Army pilot to solo was Lieutenant Frederic Humphreys, on October 26, 1909, at College Park, Maryland. He made two circuits of the field in three minutes. He was followed by Lieutenant Frank Lahm who flew six times around the field, remaining aloft for 13 minutes.

47. Who was the first American President to fly? The first American President to fly, although a former president, was Theodore Roosevelt on October 11, 1910. Roosevelt flew as a passenger with Arch Hoxsey in a Wright Model B at an air meet in St. Louis.

48. Who was the first aviator to fly a mile high? The first aviator to fly to a height of at least one mile was Walter Brookins on July 9, 1910. Brookins reached 6175 feet in his Wright Model B over Atlantic City, New Jersey.

49. Who made the first two-way radio communication between an airplane in flight and the ground? The first radio communication between an airplane in flight and the ground was made by Elmo Pickerill on August 4, 1910. Flying a Wright Model B from Mineola, Long Island, New York, Pickerill established communication with a ground station while over Manhattan Beach, Brooklyn.

50. Who was the first airplane passenger? The first passenger ever to be carried in an airplane was Charles Furnas, who was carried aloft by Wilbur Wright on May 14, 1908. The flight covered about ½ mile in 30 seconds. Later the same day Wright flew Furnas for about 2.5 miles in 4 minutes, 2 seconds. Furnas sat on top of the lower wing, next to Wilbur Wright, holding on to a strut.

51. Who was the first person to fly the English Channel? The first man to successfully fly the English Channel was Louis Blériot of France on July 25, 1909. Competing for the *Daily Mail* prize of 1000 pounds, Blériot flew a Model XI monoplane of his own design from Calais to Dover, covering the 22 miles in about fifty minutes.

52. What was the first American monoplane to fly? A monoplane designed and built by Dr. Henry Walden successfully took to the air on December 9, 1909, at Mineola, Long Island, New York. It was the third aircraft built by Walden and was powered by a 22-hp Anzani engine.

53. Who was the first to fly an airplane at night? The first recorded night flight was made in Great Britain by the Englishman Claude Grahame-White on the night of April 27–28, 1910. Grahame-White, piloting a Farman biplane, was attempting to overtake Frenchman Louis Paulhan during an air race from London to Manchester.

54. When was the world's first mid-air collision? The first mid-air collision occurred on October 3, 1910, during an aviation meet in Milan, Italy. The crash, between Bertram Dickson in a Farman, and Henri Thomas in an Antoinette, resulted in Dickson being severely injured and the Frenchman escaping unhurt. The crash occurred at an altitude of about 100 feet and both aircraft fell to earth immediately.

55. Who made the first nonstop flight from London to Paris? The first nonstop flight between these two capitols was made on April 12, 1911, by Pierre Prier in 3 hours, 56 minutes while flying a Blériot monoplane. Prier was chief instructor at the Blériot School at Hendon, England.

56. What was the first airplane to carry three passengers at once? The first airplane to carry three passengers was a Curtiss pusher biplane flown on August 14, 1910, at Mineola, New York, by Charles Foster Willard. The passengers were R. F. Patterson, A. Albin and Harry Willard. The aircraft weighed 650 pounds and the passengers and pilot weighed 550 pounds.

57. Who was the first licensed American woman pilot? The first American woman to receive a pilot's license was Harriet Quimby of New York City. Quimby received her pilot's license at the Moisant School at the Hempstead Plains Aerodrome on Long Island, New York on August 2, 1911. Quimby, a socialite reporter, was also later the first woman to fly the English Channel, on April 16, 1912. She was killed at the Harvard–Boston Air Meet in 1912.

58. What was the first airplane purchased by the U.S. Government? A Wright biplane was purchased by the U.S. Government (Army) on August 2, 1909. After successful trials at Fort Myer, Virginia, the aircraft was purchased for a price of $25,000 with a $5000 bonus as it was able to exceed 40 mph by a certain amount. Built in Dayton, Ohio, the aircraft was a refinement of the Wright Flyer flown in 1903.

59. When was the first gun fired from an airplane? The first gun to be fired from an airplane was a rifle fired by Lieutenant Jacob Fickel from a Curtiss biplane piloted by Glenn Curtiss on August 20, 1910. The military demonstration took place during an air meet at Sheepshead Bay,

Brooklyn. Fickel fired at a target on the ground during several passes, successfully striking it.

60. What was the first airplane to carry a machine gun? The first airplane to carry a machine gun was a Wright biplane flown by Lieutenant Thomas DeWitt Milling at College Park, Maryland on May 7, 1912. The gunner, armed with a Lewis Machine Gun, was Charles deForest Chandler of the U.S. Army Signal Corps. The gun was successfully fired at targets on the ground.

61. What was the first aircraft to land on the White House lawn? The first plane to land on the White House lawn was a Wright Model B flown by Harry Atwood on July 14, 1911. Atwood was presented with the Gold Medal of the Aero Club of Washington by President William Howard Taft.

62. When did an aircraft first rescue another at sea? The first rescue at sea of one airplane by another occurred on August 14, 1911, in Lake Michigan. Pilot René Simon was forced to land on the lake due to engine failure. He was spotted by Hugh Robinson who was flying over in his Curtiss Hydroaeroplane. Robinson hailed a motorboat, who then towed Simon and his plane back to shore.

63. What was the first inter-city airplane race in America? The first inter-city airplane race in America was held on August 5, 1911, between New York and Philadelphia. Three Curtiss Model Ds left Governors Island, New York, headed for Philadelphia. Lincoln Beachey won the race, as he covered the 83 miles in 1 hour, 50 minutes. Hugh Robinson came in second at 2 hours, 8 minutes, while Eugene Ely was forced to land in New Jersey.

64. What was the world's first four-engined airplane? The first four-engined aircraft in the world was the Sikorsky Grand of 1913. Built in St. Petersburg, Russia, the huge 9000 pound biplane evolved into a bomber type during World War I. It first flew on May 13, 1913 and proved to be reliable and stable. In August 1913 it set a new record with a flight of nearly two hours carrying eight people.

65. What was the first airplane sold commercially in the United States? The first commercial airplane sold in the United States was the Herring-Curtiss *Golden Flyer* built in Hammondsport, New York. The aircraft was sold to the New York Aeronautic Society, then based at the Morris Park Racetrack, Bronx, New York for $5000 in June 1909. As the racetrack confines were too small for safe flying, Glenn Curtiss selected a new site to fly on the flat, open Hempstead Plains in Nassau County, Long Island, New York. There, on July 17, 1909, Curtiss circled the airfield for 30 minutes in the *Golden Flyer,* thus winning the *Scientific American* trophy for the first flight of 25 kilometers.

66. What was the first lawsuit in the aviation industry? The first legal action in the aviation industry was when the Wright Company sued Glenn Curtiss on September 30, 1909 for patent infringement. The Wrights claimed that Curtiss utilized their patented three-axis control system without paying royalties. The legal battle ended only by the adoption of a cross-licensing agreement in 1917.

67. Who was the first person ever issued a summons for illegal flying? The first person ever issued a summons for illegal flying was Mathilde Moisant at Mineola, New York on September 25, 1911. Moisant, flying a Blériot, was issued a summons for flying on a Sunday. The Hempstead Justice, finding no prohibition on flying, dismissed the charge and "henceforth the practice of flying on Sunday" was considered legal.

68. When was the first air cargo flight? On November 7, 1910, a Wright Model B carried two bolts of dress silk, the first recorded carrying of freight by air. Phil Parmalee was the pilot and he flew from Simms Station (Dayton), Ohio to Columbus—65 miles—in 1 hour, 6 minutes.

69. When was the first airmail flight in the United States? The first official airmail flight in the United States took place on September 23, 1911. Earle Ovington (Air Mail Pilot #1), flying a Blériot monoplane, carried a 30-pound mail sack from Garden City, New York, to Mineola, New York. The three-mile flight took place during the Nassau Boulevard Air Meet as a demonstration of the future practical usage of the airplane. Ovington carried the mailbag on his lap, and dropped it over the side when he passed over the Mineola Post Office.

70. What was the world's first seaplane? The world's first seaplane was built by Henri Fabre of France, and it first flew on March 28, 1910, near Marseilles. Fabre explained that he built a seaplane rather than a landplane because he believed it would be gentler on the pilot to crash on water rather than on land. The first practical seaplane, however, was built by Glenn Curtiss and first flew in San Diego Harbor on January 26, 1911.

71. What was the world's first airline? The first (lighter than air) airline in the world to carry passengers was Delag, founded in Germany in

1910. Delag used Zeppelin airships, beginning with the *Deutschland* in 1910 and followed by four new dirigibles through 1914. Each of the 500-foot long airships could carry 20 passengers in comparative luxury. By the time the airline ended, with the beginning of World War I, it had carried over 37,000 passengers without a single injury.

72. What was the first airplane to be successfully catapulted? The first airplane to be successfully catapulted was a Curtiss Hydroaeroplane on November 12, 1912. The airplane was piloted by Lieutenant Theodore Ellyson and it was catapulted from the Washington Navy Yard over the Potomac River.

73. Who was the first paying airline passenger? Sadly, the name of the first paying airplane passenger is lost to history. However the flight occurred in England on May 17, 1911, when James Martin carried a passenger (for three pounds) from Brooklands to Hendon in a Farman biplane.

74. When did an airplane first take off from a ship? On November 14, 1910, a Curtiss Model D biplane, flown by Eugene Ely, took off from an 83-foot-long platform built on the American cruiser USS *Alabama.* The flight occurred at Hampton Roads, Virginia. With only 57 feet of the platform ahead of him, Ely staggered off with the plane actually touching the water right after takeoff. He landed safely on shore, 2½ miles away.

75. When did an airplane first land on a ship? The first airplane to land on a ship was also a Curtiss Model D, again piloted by Eugene Ely. On January 18th, 1911, Ely landed on a 120-foot-long platform constructed on the American cruiser USS *Pennsylvania,* anchored in San Francisco Bay. Despite landing downwind, Ely brought the plane to a stop after rolling only 40 feet. Sandbags holding ropes taut slowed the plane after landing. After lunch with the captain, Ely successfully took off and returned to an airfield near San Francisco.

76. What was America's first scheduled airline? America's first regularly scheduled airline started operation across Tampa Bay, Florida, between St. Petersburg and Tampa, on January 1, 1914. For the fifteen-minute flight the airline used one Benoist flying boat with Tony Jannus as pilot, carrying one passenger at a time for $5. The operation lasted three months.

77. What was the first military message delivered by airplane? The first military dispatch sent by airplane was delivered by Harry Harkness in his Antoinette on February 7, 1911. The flight was from San Diego, California, to an encampment of U.S. troops on the border near Tijuana, Mexico—a distance of 21 miles flown in 25 minutes.

78. When was the first air raid? The world's first air raid occurred on November 1, 1911, when Italian Lieutenant Giulio Gavotti dropped a five-pound bomb on a Turkish position in Libya during the Italo-Turkish War of 1911–1912. Gavotti, flying an Etrich monoplane, took off from Tripoli and attacked the Turkish camp at Ain Zura. The raid brought strong protests from the Turks, who claimed the Italians were contravening the Geneva Convention.

79. Who was the first casualty in aerial warfare? The first casualty in aerial warfare occurred on March 31, 1912, when a Captain Montu was wounded by gunfire from an Arab encampment at Tobruk while in the process of dropping bombs from the observer's seat. The aircraft was flown by Lieutenant Rossi at an altitude of 1800 feet when four bullets struck the fuselage, one of them hitting Montu.

80. Who was the first pilot shot down and killed? The first pilot to be killed in a war was a Bulgarian, M. Popoff, on November 3, 1912. Popoff was shot down while making a reconnaissance flight over Adrianople.

81. Who was the first person to make a parachute jump from an airplane in America? The first parachute jump from an airplane in America was made by Captain Albert Berry on March 1, 1912. Berry jumped from a Benoist aircraft flown by Anthony Jannus at 1500 feet, near St. Louis, Missouri.

82. When was the world's first automatic pilot demonstrated? The first gyroscopic automatic stabilizer (autopilot) for an aircraft was successfully demonstrated by Lawrence Sperry (son of inventor Elmer Sperry) in August 1913. Sperry demonstrated the device in a Curtiss Model F flying boat, and in 1914 he repeated the "hands off" demonstration in France to win a prize for the first automatically stablized aircraft.

83. Who was the first person to loop an airplane? The first pilot in the world to perform a loop was Lieutenant Petr Nesterov of the Imperial Russian Air Service. He performed it on August 20, 1913, at Kiev, flying a Nieuport Type IV.

84. What was the first known aerial combat? The first known aerial combat occurred on December 4, 1913, over Naco, Mexico. Phil Rader, flying a Curtiss pusher for the Mexican government, engaged Dean Lamb, flying another Curtiss for rebel forces. Both men exchanged pistol shots without success.

85. Who made the first coast-to-coast flight in an airplane? The first transcontinental aircraft flight in America was made by Cal Rodgers in a Wright EX between September 17 and November 5, 1911. Rodgers was attempting to win a prize offered by William Randolph Hearst for the first transcontinental flight in 30 days or less. Rodgers took 49 days, but he completed the flight just to be the first to do so. The flight was between Sheepshead Bay, Brooklyn, and Long Beach, California. Actual flying time was 3 days, 10 hours, 14 minutes.

World War I

86. What was the world's first all-metal airplane? The world's first successful all-metal airplane was the Junkers J-1 built in Dessau, Germany in 1915. Initiated as a private project by Professor Hugo Junkers, the plane's first flight was made on December 12, 1915. The aircraft, complete with corrugated metal skin, had a top speed of 105 mph and served as the prototype for later models of Junkers all-metal aircraft built during World War I.

87. What was the world's first capitol to be bombed? The first bombs to be dropped on a capitol city fell on Paris on August 30, 1914. Lieutenant Ferdinand Von Hiddessen of the Imperial German Air Service, flying a Taube monoplane, dropped two bombs, killing two French civilians.

88. What was the first airplane to be shot down in World War I? The first airplane in World War I to be shot down was a German two-seat Aviatik over Rheims, France on October 5, 1914. The aircraft was shot down by Frenchman Joseph Frantz in a Voisin pusher. The weapon used was a Hotchkiss machine gun mounted in the front cockpit.

89. When were American aircraft first used in combat? The first American army aircraft to actually be used on a military expedition were eight Curtiss JNs of the 1st Aero Squadron, U.S. Army. The aircraft were part of a military expedition to Mexico under General John Pershing in March 1916 in search of the bandit, Pancho Villa.

90. What were the first American aircraft to see combat in World War I? The first American-built aircraft to go overseas and see combat were five LWF V-1s built in College Point, Queens, New York. The aircraft served on the eastern front with the fledgling Czech Air Force in their war against Russia, beginning in the summer of 1917.

91. Who was the first American shot down in World War I? The first American aviator shot down and killed in World War I was H. Clyde Balsey, on June 18, 1916. Balsey was flying for the Lafayette Escadrille (American volunteers fighting for France) when he was shot down in his Nieuport near Verdun.

92. Who was the first American to score an aerial victory in World War I?
The first American to score a "kill" in World War I was Kiffin Rockwell, flying a Nieuport for the French Lafayette Escadrille, on May 8, 1916. Rockwell shot down a German reconnaissance plane over Thann, France.

93. Who was the first woman military pilot? The first woman military pilot was Princess Eugenie Mikhailovna Shakovskaya of Russia. She learned to fly in Germany in 1911, and when World War I broke out in 1914, she made a personal request to the Tsar that she be allowed to serve as a military pilot. In November 1914 she was posted to the 1st Field Air Squadron as a reconnaissance pilot. She survived the war.

94. Who was the first American to score an aerial victory in an American unit? The first American in an American unit to shoot down an enemy aircraft was Lieutenant Stephen Thompson of the First Aero Squadron. He scored his first victory on February 5, 1918, at Saarbrucken, Germany, when he downed an Albatross fighter.

95. What was the first use of airborne radio in combat? The first use of airborne radio in combat occurred on September 24, 1914, by Lieutenants D. S. Lewis and B. T. James of No. 4 Squadron, Royal Flying Corps. They directed artillery fire from the air during the First Battle of the Aisne from their BE-2. Both officers were killed in action shortly thereafter.

96. What was the first true fighter plane? The first true fighter plane, that is, one firing a machine gun straight ahead through the propeller, was a French Morane-Saulnier monoplane flown by Roland Garros. On April 1, 1915, Garros shot down a German machine by firing his gun through his propeller which was equipped with metal deflector plates.

97. When did naval aircraft first see combat? The first naval aircraft to engage in combat were Japanese Farman biplane seaplanes flying from the seaplane tender, *Wakamiya,* on September 1, 1914. The Japanese planes attacked German forces at Kiaochow Bay, China, dropping improvised bombs made from naval shells. They succeeded in sinking a German minelayer in the action.

98. When was the first ship sunk by a torpedo dropped from an airplane? A ship was first successfully attacked by an aircraft torpedo on August 17, 1915. On that day Royal Navy Lieutenant G. B. Dacre, flying a Short 184, was forced to land on the water, just north of the Dardanelles, due to engine trouble. Upon seeing a Turkish tugboat close by, he taxied up to it and released his torpedo. The tugboat blew up and sank, whereupon Dacre was able to eventually take off and return to his ship.

99. What was the first ship to be called an aircraft carrier? The first vessel in the world to be called an aircraft carrier was the British light battlecruiser HMS *Furious*. Begun early in World War I as a cruiser, in 1917 her design was altered and she was completed with a hangar and flight deck. She carried six Sopwith Pups as well as four seaplanes. On August 2, 1917, Squadron Leader E.H. Dunning made the world's first landing on a ship underway. Regrettably, on August 7, Dunning was killed while attempting his second landing.

100. When was the first air raid on England? The first air raid on England, also the first raid by Zeppelins, was made on the night of January 19, 1915. The German Navy Zeppelins L3 and L4 dropped just over a ton of bombs on Great Yarmouth, Kings Lynn, and smaller places in Norfolk. The raid killed four civilians and injured sixteen. Military damage was insignificant, but wild enthusiasm prevailed in Germany. In England there was horror, shock, and outrage from the press, government, and civil populace.

101. Who was the first person to shoot down a Zeppelin? The first person to shoot down a Zeppelin was Lieutenant William Leefe Robinson of the British Home Defence Force. On the night of September 2–3, 1916, 16 German airships made night raids across England. The Army airship Shutte-Lanz SL-11 was spotted by Robinson, flying a BE-2C. After overtaking the airship, Robinson fired three drums of ammunition into it from his Lewis gun, setting it on fire. She fell burning on Cuffley, all 16 of her crew were killed.

102. Who was the leading ace of World War I? The greatest ace of World War I, with the most aerial victories, was the German Manfred Von Richthofen, often known as the "Red Baron." Between September 1916 and April 1918, Von Richthofen was credited with 80 victories, and was awarded his country's highest decoration. A cold, calculating aristocrat, Von Richthofen preferred to fly the unstable, but highly manueverable, Fokker DR1 triplane. He was ultimately shot down on April 21, 1918, by Captain Roy Brown of the RFC, after straying far over enemy lines.

103. Who was the greatest allied ace of World War I? The greatest allied ace of the First World War was Captain René Fonck of France. Fonck is credited with 75 victories, but he may have had up to 25 more which were unconfirmed. Unlike most World War I aviators, Fonck died peacefully in his sleep in Paris in 1953. A thoughtful and analytical pilot, Fonck frequently shot down an airplane with the expenditure of less than ten rounds.

104. Who was America's greatest ace of World War I? The most successful American pilot of the First World War was Captain Edward V. Rickenbacker, who shot down 26 German aircraft. Prior to the war, Rickenbacker was one of America's leading racecar drivers. Rickenbacker did not get to see frontline service until March, 1918, when he secured a transfer to the 94th Aero Squadron, and he was grounded from June through September with an ear infection. His last 21 "kills" occurred in the last eight weeks of the war.

105. What was the largest aircraft built during World War I? The largest aircraft of World War I was a bomber, the Siemens Schukert R. VIII, with a 158-foot wingspan. Begun in 1916, the advanced R. VIII featured an enclosed revolving turret, six 300-hp engines, and trim tabs on its control surfaces. Only one example was built and it never saw combat. The aircraft was to be a carrier for wire-guided flying bombs the Germans were developing.

The Golden Age
1919–1939

106. What was the first municipal airport in the United States? The first municipal airport in the United States was at Atlantic City, New Jersey. Dedicated on May 3, 1918, the airport (greatly expanded) still exists as Bader Field.

107. When was regular airmail service begun in the United States? Regular airmail service in the United States began May 15, 1918, when two Curtiss JN-4s (top speed 40 mph) departed from Washington D.C. and Belmont Park, New York, each headed for the other city. The flight from Washington was made by Army Lieutenant Torrey Webb, who was forced to land in Maryland, the first day's mail reaching its destination by train.

108. Who made the first transatlantic flight? A Navy Curtiss flying boat called the NC-4 made the first crossing of the Atlantic by air. Commanded by A. C. Read, with a crew of five, the huge flying boat departed Rockaway, Long Island, on May 8, 1919. After stopping at Halifax, Newfoundland, the Azores, and Lisbon, the NC-4 arrived at Plymouth, England on May 31. Total distance flown was 3925 miles in 57 hours of flying time at an average speed of 68 mph.

109. What was the first nonstop flight across the Atlantic Ocean? The first nonstop flight across the Atlantic Ocean took place on June 14–15, 1919, when Captain John Alcock and Lt. Arthur Brown flew a British Vickers Vimy bomber from St. John's, Newfoundland, to Clifden, Ireland. Powered by two Rolls Royce engines, the 1936-mile flight took nearly 16 hours. Both men were knighted for their achievement.

110. What was the first airship (lighter than air) to fly the Atlantic Ocean? The first airship crossing of the Atlantic, and also the first east-to-west flight, was made by the British rigid airship R-34 between July 2–6, 1919. Commanded by L. H. Scott, with a crew of 30, the R-34 departed East Fortune, Scotland and flew to Roosevelt Field, Long Island. After two days in New York, the airship flew back to England, making this the first round-trip crossing of the Atlantic. Total distance covered was 6330 miles in 183 hours, 8 minutes. On the westward leg, the R-34 also carried the first aeronautical stowaway, William Ballantyne, a rigger who was eliminated from the crew to save weight, but who did not want to be left behind.

111. When was the first wedding in an airplane? The first wedding in an airplane took place on May 31, 1919, in a converted Handley Page bomber. Flying at 2000 feet over Ellington Field, Texas, Marjorie Dumont and Lieutenant R. W. Meade were married by an army chaplain.

112. Who made the first free-fall parachute jump in the United States? The first free-fall parachute jump from an airplane in the United States was made by Leslie Irving at McCook Field, Dayton, Ohio on April 28, 1919. Irving leapt from an Air Service DH-9 flown by Floyd Smith, designer of the parachute.

113. When was the first transcontinental air race? The first transcontinental air race began on October 8, 1919. On that day 15 airplanes left San Francisco and 48 left Roosevelt Field, New York on a 5400-mile round-trip race across the continent sponsored by the American Flying Club of New York. The race was won by Lieutenant Belvin Maynard, flying a DH-4, who left Roosevelt Field and arrived in San Francisco 3 days, 6 hours later. His return trip took 3 days, 21 hours.

114. What was the first airliner with a radio? The first airliner with a radio was an Aircraft Transport & Travel Ltd. DH-42 that went into service in June 1919. Flying between London and Paris, the aircraft was equipped with a AD 1/s radio set installed by the Marconi company.

115. What was the first ship specifically designed and built as an aircraft carrier? The first ship ever specifically designed and built as an aircraft carrier was the 7470-ton displacement *Hosho,* built for the Japanese Navy. The ship's keel was laid down on December 19, 1919, and it began sea trials off Tateyama on November 30, 1922. She carried 21 aircraft and had a maximum speed of 25 knots.

116. What airplane had the first fully retractable landing gear? The world's first airplane with a fully retractable landing gear was the Dayton-Wright RB racing monoplane of 1920. Built for the Gordon Bennett Aviation Trophy Race, the aircraft was a remarkably advanced design featuring retractable landing gear, variable camber wings, and a top speed of 200 mph. It was forced to withdraw from the Bennett race due to engine problems.

117. When was the first Intercollegiate Air Meet? The first Intercollegiate Air Meet was held May 7, 1920, at Mitchel Field, New

York. Conducted under the auspices of the U.S. Air Service, all participating students flew Army Curtiss JN-4 "Jennies." Of the 11 colleges participating, Yale University won with nine points.

118. When was the first coast-to-coast airmail flight? The first coast-to-coast airmail flight was made February 22–23, 1921. Jack Knight, in a DeHavilland DH-4, flew from San Francisco to Roosevelt Field, New York in 33 hours, 20 minutes.

119. What was the first American airline to fly between the United States and a foreign country? The first American airline to fly between the U.S. and a foreign country was Aeromarine Airways in February 1920. Using converted Curtiss F5L flying boats, Aeromarine carried passengers between Key West, Florida, and Havana, Cuba. Fourteen passengers could be carried at a time in two separate compartments.

120. What was the first airliner with a toilet? The first airliner with a toilet was a DeHavilland DH-34 belonging to Diamler Airlines, England. Diamler began service in August 1920 between Paris and London. Their single-engine DH-34s could carry eight passengers.

121. Who was the first person to reach 35,000 feet in an airplane? The first person to reach an altitude of 35,000 feet was Curtiss test pilot Roland Rohlfs. On September 18, 1919, over Curtiss Field, Long Island, he reached that altitude in an open cockpit Curtiss 18T triplane. He sucked on a tube from an oxygen bottle so he could breathe at that altitude.

122. What was the first trimotored airliner? The first three-engined airliner was the Curtiss Eagle, built shortly after World War I. On October 24, 1919, an Eagle carried eight passengers from Garden City, Long Island, New York, to Washington, D.C.

123. When was an airplane first used in a political campaign? The first time an aircraft was used for a political campaign was October 31, 1920. On that day a Curtiss JN-4 bombarded Toledo, Ohio with socialist literature on behalf of candidate Eugene V. Debs.

124. When was a battleship first sunk by airplanes? The first battleship ever sunk by airplanes was the *Ostfriesland,* a former German battleship. The sinking took place on July 21, 1921, near Hampton Roads, Virginia, during a bombing demonstration conducted by General William Mitchell. Martin bombers at first made three hits out of five with 1000-pound bombs, and later the ship was sunk with seven 2000-pound bombs. The ship sank 21 minutes after the second attack began.

125. When was the first mid-air collision between airliners? The first mid-air collision between airliners took place on April 7, 1922, between a Diamler Airways DH-18 and a Grand Express Aériens Farman Goliath. Both aircraft were following the same road on reciprocal courses and collided 18 miles north of Beauvais, France. All nine aboard were killed.

126. When was the first coast-to-coast crossing of the United States in a single day? The first crossing of the U.S. in a single day was made on September 4, 1922, by Lieutenant James Doolittle flying an improved DH-4B from Pablo Beach, Florida to Rockwell Field, San Diego. The 2163-mile flight took 21 hours, 20 minutes, including a short refueling stop in Texas.

127. Who was the first woman to make a transcontinental flight as a passenger? The first woman passenger on a transcontinental flight was Lillian Gatlin of Santa Ana, California. Between October 5 and 8, 1922, she flew between San Francisco and Mineola, New York, in a U.S. Post Office DH-4. The 2680-mile nine-stop flight took 27 hours, 11 minutes flying time.

128. What was the first airplane to land at the U.S. Capitol? The first airplane to land at the U.S. Capitol was a Sperry Messenger, flown by Lawrence Sperry. On March 23, 1922, Sperry landed on the concrete plaza in front of the Capitol and turned the plane up the Capitol steps to stop, as it had no brakes. The small scout plane weighed 500 pounds and had a wingspan of 20 feet.

129. When was the first air-to-air refueling of an aircraft? The first successful air-to-air refueling took place on June 27, 1923, over San Diego. Captain L. H. Smith and Lieutenant J. P. Richter in a DH-4B were refueled by another DH-4 lowering a fuel line in preparation for an endurance record attempt. On August 27–28, they stayed aloft for 37 hours, 15 minutes, to set a new world endurance record. In that effort they were air-to-air refueled 15 times.

130. What was the first illuminated airway? The first illuminated airway was the Chicago to Cheyenne route, which was switched on on August 21, 1923. Forty-two landing fields on the route were lit by 30, 6-inch electric arc beacons. The lights of 5.3 million candlepower were visible for 50 miles.

131. What was the first widely used civilian lightplane? The first widely used civilian lightplane was the British DH Moth, designed by Geoffrey deHavilland in 1924. The two-seat wood and fabric biplane first flew in February 1925, and initially sold for 650 pounds. The Moth was used to establish a state-subsidized flying club movement in Britain that was copied in many countries. About 2000 Moths were built, followed by about 9200 of a more developed version, the Tiger Moth.

132. What was the first six-engined American aircraft? The first six-engined American aircraft was the Barling XNBL-1, first flown in 1923. Powered by six 420-hp Liberty engines, this huge experimental long-range bomber had a wingspan of 120 feet and a maximum loaded weight of 42,569 pounds. Unfortunately its huge fuel consumption and slow speed gave it a range of only 170 miles with a bomb load. Built at a cost of $350,000, the project was abandoned after only one was built.

133. When was the first nonstop crossing of the United States by air? The first nonstop air crossing of the United States took place on May 2–3, 1923. Lieutenants O. G. Kelly and J. A. Macready, flying an Air Service Fokker T-2, took off from Roosevelt Field, Long Island and arrived at Rockwell Field, San Diego, 26 hours, 50 minutes later. The distance flown was 2520 miles.

134. What was the first American-built rigid airship? The first American-built rigid airship was the ZR-1, named the *Shenandoah,* commissioned on August 20, 1923 at Lakehurst, New Jersey. Commanded by Lt. Commander Zachery Lansdowne, it was destroyed in a thunderstorm on September 3, 1925, over Caldwell, Ohio. Lansdowne and 14 members of the crew were killed.

135. What were the first airplanes to fly around the world? The first successful around-the-world flight was accomplished by two Douglas "World Cruisers" (modified Navy torpedo bombers) between April 6 and September 28, 1924. Four airplanes started the journey from Seattle, but two were lost to crashes enroute. The aircraft made a total of 58 stops and flew a total of 27,553 miles. The flight took a total of 175 days, with a flying time of 365 hours.

136. When were troops first airlifted? The first time soldiers were airlifted was April 1923 during the Kurdish uprising. A fully-equipped fighting force of 280 Sikh troops were flown by the RAF from Kingarban, Iraq to Kirkuk, Iraq, in 12-seat Vickers Vernon transports. The time taken to transport the whole force the 75-mile distance was a day and a half, or about 10 flying hours. The journey normally would have taken five days march.

137. What was the first airplane inspected by the Federal Government?
The first airplane inspected by the Federal Government (the Commerce Department) was a Stinson Detroiter being delivered to Canadian Air Express. It was inspected by Ralph Lockwood of the Aeronautics Branch on December 7, 1926. It passed.

138. Where was the first air passenger international arrivals building? The first air passenger international arrivals building was established at Meacham Field, Key West, Florida on October 28, 1927. The first flight from the station was made by Pan American Airways to Havana, Cuba.

139. What was the first aircraft noise complaint reported to the Aeronautics Branch of the Commerce Department? On January 31, 1928, the proprietor of the Cackle Corner Poultry Farm, Garrettsville, Ohio, complained that low-flying planes were disrupting egg production. The Commerce Department suggested to National Air Transport, the private company operating the New York to Chicago airmail route, that its planes make a special effort to maintain altitude over Garrettsville.

140. Who made the first east-to-west crossing of the Atlantic Ocean by air? The first east-to-west crossing of the Atlantic was made by Baron Guenther Von Huenefeld, Captain Hermann Koehl, and Major James Fitzmaurice on April 12–13, 1928. They took off from Baldonell, Ireland in the Junkers *Bremen* and made a forced landing on Greenley Island, Canada, 37 hours later.

141. Who made the first transpacific flight? The first transpacific flight was made by Captain Charles Kingsford Smith and the crew of the *Southern Cross,* a Fokker F. VIIB-3. The flight was made from San Francisco to Brisbane, Australia in four stops, between May 31 and June 9, 1928.

142. When did the first aviation weather Teletype go into operation? The first aviation weather Teletype went into operation on July 1, 1928. On that day, stations at Cleveland, Ohio, and Chicago, Illinois, received weather reports from a central office in Washington, D.C. By October 1938, the Teletype weather communications system had been extended to a total of 21,790 miles, covering all 48 states except South Dakota.

143. When was the first coast-to-coast air passenger service inaugurated? The first coast-to-coast air passenger service was inaugurated on July 7, 1929. Passengers flew by Ford Trimotor by day and rode trains at night. The 48-hour cross-country service was begun by Transcontinental Air Transport (later TWA), and the first plane was flown by Charles Lindbergh.

144. What was the first airport with radio air traffic control? The first airport with radio air traffic control was Cleveland Municipal, beginning on May 15, 1930. In the next five years approximately 20 cities were to follow Cleveland's lead.

145. When did the first plane fly between the United States mainland and Hawaii? The first flight between the U.S. mainland and Hawaii was achieved by Lieutenants Albert Hegenberger and Lester Maitland on June 28–29, 1927. Flying an Army Fokker C-2 trimotor, the *Bird of Paradise,* the 2407-mile flight from Oakland, California to Honolulu, Hawaii took 25 hours, 50 minutes.

146. When were the first movies shown in an aircraft? Motion pictures were first shown in an aircraft in flight on October 8, 1929. On that day a current newsreel and two cartoon comedies were shown on a Transcontinental Air Transport Ford Trimotor flying at 5000 feet. The special movie projector weighed only eight pounds.

147. What was the first all metal dirigible? The first airship made completely of metal was the Navy ZMC-2, which was made by the Detroit Aircraft Corporation. It was first flown in Michigan on August 19, 1929, and was manned by a crew of five. The dirigible was 149-feet long and carried 202,000 cubic feet of helium. It weighed 9115 pounds empty, with a gross weight of 12,245 pounds. The airship, with its thin aluminum skin, made 752 successful flights for the U.S. Navy before being scrapped in 1942.

148. What was the first American aircraft carrier? The first American aircraft carrier commissioned for fleet service was the USS *Langley,* which began life as a freighter called the *Jupiter.* Completed in 1922, the first pilot to take off from her was Commander Virgil Griffin on October 17 of that year. Griffin was flying a Vought VE-7. The *Langley* could carry a total of 34 aircraft.

149. Who made the world's first rocket-powered airplane? The world's first rocket-plane was built by Rhon-Rossitten Gesellschaft of Germany. It first flew on June 11, 1928, piloted by Friedrich Stamer. The powered canard glider *Duck* was carried aloft by two Sander solid-fuel rockets and flew ¾ of a mile at a speed of about 70 mph. On September 30, 1928, Fritz Von Opel flew a rocket-powered glider near Frankfurt, and this is often stated as being the world's first rocket-plane.

150. When were the first meals cooked on an airliner? The first meals cooked on an airliner were served on an Imperial Airways (England) flight on May 1, 1927. The flight, from London to Paris, was made in an Armstrong Whitworth Argosy carrying 18 passengers.

151. What was the world's first airline crash? The world's first airline crash occurred on December 14, 1920, at Golders Green, just north of London. The airliner, of Handley Page Continental Air Services, had just taken off for Paris with a crew of two and six passengers. It crashed into the back of a house off the end of the runway, killing four and injuring two.

152. When did an airplane first fly over the North Pole? The first airplane flight over the North Pole was made by Lt. Commander Richard Byrd and Floyd Bennett on May 9, 1926. They flew a trimotored Fokker, the *Josephine Ford,* over the Pole from their base at Spitsbergen, Norway.

153. When was the first flight over the South Pole? The first flight over the South Pole was made by Commander Richard Byrd, Bernt Balchen, Captain R. Ashley, C. McKinley, and Harold June on November 28, 1928. They were flying a Ford Trimotor, the *Floyd Bennett,* from their basecamp at "Little America" in Antarctica.

154. What was the first airplane launched from a submarine? The first airplane to be launched from a submarine was a Navy Cox-Klemin XS-1 on July 27, 1923 at the Washington Navy Yard. The tiny scout plane, with folding wings, was designed to fit in a watertight tube carried on the submarine's deck.

155. What was the first airplane with hydraulic landing gear struts? The first airplane with an oleo-type hydraulic strut was a Navy NB-1 first tested on April 13, 1925, in Seattle, Washington. The oleo gear soon proved to be far superior to the old type bungee cord then in general use.

156. Who was the first person to do an "outside" loop? The first person to accomplish an outside loop in an airplane was Lieutenant James Doolittle in an Army Racer on May 25, 1927.

157. Who was the first woman to fly the Atlantic? The first woman to fly the Atlantic Ocean was Amelia Earhart on June 17–18, 1928. She was a passenger on the Fokker trimotor, *Friendship,* flown by Wilmer Stultz and Lew Gordon from Trepassey Bay, Newfoundland to Burry Port, Wales.

158. Who made the first solo transatlantic flight? The first solo transatlantic flight, as well as the first flight from New York to Paris, was made by Charles A. Lindbergh on May 20–21, 1927. Responding to a $25,000 prize offered by Raymond Orteig in 1919, Lindbergh was one of several contenders attempting to be the first to fly between America and Europe nonstop. A 25-year-old airmail pilot, Lindbergh planned his flight meticulously. The airplane he selected was a Ryan monoplane, the *Spirit of St. Louis,* an improved version of their M-1 mailplane, powered by a 220-hp Wright J-5 engine. Lindbergh departed Roosevelt Field, Long Island and successfully arrived at LeBourget airport, Paris, 33 hours, 30 minutes later. The flight revolutionized and popularized aviation as nothing else before or since.

159. Who was the first person to make a completely "blind flight" in an airplane? The world's first "blind flight" including takeoff and landing, was made by Lieutenant James Doolittle on September 24, 1929. Flying a Consolidated NY-2 Husky equipped with newly developed instrumentation, including a Kollsman sensitive altimeter and Sperry artificial horizon, Doolittle took off from Mitchel Field, New York, flew a prescribed course, and landed, solely on instruments. Doolittle's cockpit was covered with a hood so he had no outside visibility. The flight soon led to safer commercial aircraft which could fly at night and in poor weather.

160. Who was the first municipally-employed air traffic controller? The first municipally-employed air traffic controller was Archie League, who went to work at Lambert Field, St. Louis, in May 1929. League's "control tower" was a wheelbarrow that he used to haul his flags from one runway to another in order to regulate takeoffs and landings.

161. When was the first baby born in an airplane? The first baby born in an airplane was born to Mrs. T. W. Evans of Miami on October 30, 1929. When Mrs. Evans went into labor, she rushed to the local airfield where her husband took her aloft along with a nurse and a doctor. At 1200 feet, a girl was born, whom the Evans' subsequently named Aerogene.

162. When was the first "snatch" airmail pickup by a plane? The first airmail pickup where planes snatch the mail from the ground without landing took place in Washington, D.C. on October 1, 1929. The pickup was part of a demonstration by Pennsylvania Central Airlines. The demonstration was repeated successfully, and eventually the system was used regularly on the Pittsburgh to Cleveland route, as well as in many rural places during the early 1930s.

163. Who was the first woman to make a transcontinental airplane flight? The first woman to make a transcontinental airplane flight was Laura Ingalls, who left Roosevelt Field, New York on October 5, 1930, in a

Moth biplane. She reached Glendale, California in 30 hours, 27 minutes flying time with nine stops. On October 18, she made a return flight to Roosevelt Field in 25 hours, 35 minutes flying time.

164. Who was the first woman to make a solo flight across the Atlantic Ocean? The first woman to make a solo flight across the Atlantic Ocean was Amelia Earhart on May 20–21, 1932. She departed Harbor Grace, Newfoundland in a Lockheed Vega 5B and landed in Londonderry, Ireland, 14 hours, 54 minutes later.

165. What was the first transpolar flight from the Soviet Union to the United States? The first transpolar flight was made by a Soviet ANT-25 on June 17–20, 1933. The aircraft was an unusually large single-engine plane, and it carried a crew of Valeri Chkalov, Georgi Baidukov, and Alexander Belyakov. The flight departed from Moscow and, after flying through appalling conditions, landed at Vancouver, Washington, 63 hours, 16 minutes later.

166. What was the first successful man-carrying aircraft powered by a steam engine? The first aircraft powered by a steam engine to fly was a Travel Air biplane. The steam engine was designed by George Besler, and the flight was made from Oakland, California, Municipal Airport on April 12, 1933.

167. What was the first aircraft equipped with radar? The first crude form of radar was tested on a light of the U.S. Navy rigid airship *Los Angeles* over New York on February 9, 1932. The device, called a sonic altimeter, emitted a sound that bounced off the ground and was heard by a stethoscope on the airship. A timer then indicated the distance to the ground.

168. What was the first airliner with an autopilot? The first time an autopilot was used on an airliner was November 10, 1931. An 18-passenger Eastern Airlines Curtiss Condor was equipped with a "mechanical co-pilot" on its flight from New York to Washington, D.C. The device was built by Sperry, and it was able to operate all flight controls of the plane except during takeoff and landing.

169. What was the first aircraft to carry 200 people? The first aircraft to carry over 200 people was the U.S. Navy rigid airship *Akron*. On November 3, 1931, it carried 207 people from Akron, Ohio, to Lakehurst, New Jersey on its delivery flight. This was the largest number of persons ever carried by a single craft in the air up to this time.

170. When was the first time live lobsters were flown on an airplane? The first time live lobsters were flown on an airplane was on June 6, 1932.

Harold Moon delivered 500 lobsters from Boston to Philadelphia in a Bellanca monoplane. The Consolidated Lobster Company of Gloucester, Massachusetts pioneered the venture.

171. Who was the first woman to make a solo east-to-west crossing of the Atlantic Ocean? The first woman to make a solo east-to-west crossing of the Atlantic Ocean was Beryl Markham of Nairobi, Kenya. She departed from Abingdon, England on September 4, 1936, in a Percival Vega Gull, *The Messenger,* and landed on Cape Breton Island, Nova Scotia. She was attempting to reach New York, but ran short of fuel.

172. When did an airship first make an around-the-world flight? The first, and only, around-the-world airship flight was made by the German *Graf Zeppelin* between August 8 and 29, 1929. Under the command of Dr. Hugo Eckener, the airship left Lakehurst, New Jersey and only stopped at Friedrichshafen, Germany; Tokyo, Japan; and Los Angeles before returning to Lakehurst. The 21-day, 7-hour flight was also the fastest around-the-world flight at the time.

173. Who was the first American airline stewardess? The first airline stewardess in the United States was Ellen Church of United Air Lines, who made her first flight on May 15, 1930, between San Francisco and Cheyenne, Wyoming in a Boeing 80A trimotor. Church, a registered nurse from Iowa, was not only required to serve the passengers, she also had to clean the plane, load baggage, sell tickets, and help refuel the plane.

174. When was the first nonstop flight between Japan and the United States? The first nonstop flight between Japan and the United States was made by Clyde Pangborn and Hugh Herndon between October 3–5, 1931. They flew between Tokyo and Wenatchee, Washington in a Bellanca monoplane.

175. What was the first airliner with beds? The first airliner with sleeping compartments was the twin-engine biplane Curtiss Condor. American Airlines began sleeper service between Chicago and New York on July 9, 1934.

176. Who was the first woman to make a nonstop transcontinental flight? The first woman to make a nonstop transcontinental flight was Amelia Earhart on August 24, 1932. She flew from Los Angeles to Newark, New Jersey in her Lockheed Vega in 19 hours, 5 minutes.

177. What was the first airplane to carry an automobile? The first airplane to carry an automobile was the Burnelli RB-2 in 1925. Hudson Motors used the plane to carry an Essex automobile on an aerial sales tour and Burnelli did it as a demonstration of the aircraft's load-carrying capabilities.

178. What was the first American monoplane fighter with enclosed cockpit and retractable landing gear? The first "modern" American fighter, all-metal, with enclosed cockpit and retractable landing gear, was the Seversky P-35. Deliveries began in July 1937 with a total of 137 going to the Air Corps. The aircraft was powered by a 950-hp Pratt & Whitney R-1830, and it had a top speed of 281 mph. The P-35 was a direct ancestor of the Famous P-47 Thunderbolt of World War II.

179. What were the only fighter planes ever carried aboard an airship? The first, and only, American fighters to serve aboard airships were U.S. Navy Curtiss F9C Sparrowhawks that served aboard the airships *Akron* and *Macon* between 1932 and 1935. The aircraft would hook on to a "trapeze" lowered from the airship in flight and then be raised up into the ship's "hangar."

180. What was the Navy's first plane to feature retractable landing gear? The first airplane with a retractable landing gear used by the U.S. Navy was the Grumman FF-1 two-place fighter. The FF-1 went into service with Navy Squadron VF-5 on June 21, 1933 on board the USS *Lexington.*

181. What was the world's first pressurized flying suit? The first pressurized flying suit, developed specifically for high-altitude flying, was that used by Wiley Post in 1934. In an effort to fly his Lockheed Vega at even greater altitudes where he could go faster, Post developed a suit, made by the B.F. Goodrich Rubber Company, that would maintain an internal pressure of 5,500 feet regardless of his actual altitude. On September 5, 1934, using this suit, Post reached nearly 40,000 feet in his plane, the *Winnie Mae.* The suit resembled that of a deep-sea diver, complete with a cylindrical metal helmet with viewing port.

182. Who made the first solo east-to-west crossing of the Atlantic Ocean? The first solo east-to-west crossing of the Atlantic Ocean was made by James Mollison on August 18–19, 1932. Flying a DeHavilland Puss Moth, *The Heart's Content,* he flew from Dublin, Ireland to Pennfield, New Brunswick.

183. Who made the first solo around-the-world flight? The first solo around-the-world flight was made by Wiley Post between July 15 and 22, 1933. Flying a Lockheed Vega, he departed and returned to Floyd Bennett Field, New York, a distance of 15,596 miles, in 7 days, 18 hours, 49 minutes. He stopped at Berlin, Moscow, Irkutsk (Siberia), and Alaska.

184. What was the first commercial flight of a pressurized airliner? The first commercial flight of a pressurized airliner was on July 8, 1940. On that day a TWA Boeing 307 "Stratoliner," carrying 33 passengers, flew from Burbank, California to LaGuardia Airport, New York, in 12 hours, 22 minutes.

185. Who was the first person to be towed across the country in a glider? The first person to be towed across the country in a glider was Captain Frank Hawks. In April 1930 he was towed from San Diego to Roosevelt Field, New York in a glider named the *Texaco Eaglet.* The 2860-mile flight took 36 hours, 47 minutes.

186. When were the world's first aerial traffic reports? The first traffic reports from the air were made from a Goodyear blimp operating out of Holmes Airport, Queens, New York during the summer of 1936.

187. What was the first control tower at a military airport? The first military control tower went into operation on October 15, 1936, at Mitchel Field, Long Island, New York. The tower was a converted greenhouse placed on the roof of the field's headquarters building.

188. What is the highest a piston-engine aircraft has ever flown? The current altitude record for piston-engine airplanes—56,046 feet—was set on October 22, 1938, by Mario Pezzi in a Caproni 161 over Montecelio, Italy. He wore a partial pressure suit filled with water, while his engine continued to run in that rarefied atmosphere despite the absence of a supercharger. This is one of the oldest records still on the books.

189. When was the first commercial transpacific flight? The first commercial transpacific flight occurred between November 22 and 28, 1935. On November 22, a Pan American Martin M-130 flying boat *China Clipper,* departed San Francisco for Manila. After overnight stops at Midway, Wake, and Guam islands, the flight arrived in the Philippines. Total flying time was 60 hours at an average speed of 143 mph.

190. What was the first commercial transatlantic aircraft flight? The first commercial transatlantic flight occurred on May 20–21, 1939. The flight was made by a Pan American Boeing 314 flying boat, *Yankee Clipper,* that departed Port Washington, Long Island, for France. Carrying only mail, the *Yankee Clipper* arrived in Marseilles 26 hours,

54 minutes after departing Port Washington, including a refueling stop in the Azores. On June 24, 1939, the first commercial passenger flight, a Pan American B-314, the *Dixie Clipper,* carrying 22 passengers, departed Port Washington for Southampton, England. The round-trip flight cost $775.

191. Who was the first President with a pilot's license? The first president with a pilot's license, #93258, was Dwight D. Eisenhower. Eisenhower earned his license on November 30, 1939, while in the army on the staff of General Douglas MacArthur in the Philippines. He allowed his license to lapse upon leaving the military.

World War II

192. What was the first successful helicopter in the United States? The first successful helicopter in the United States was the Sikorsky VS-300, which first made a tethered flight in Stratford, Connecticut on September 14, 1939. Flown by designer Igor Sikorsky, the VS-300 was powered by a 75-hp engine. It made its first successful free flight on May 14, 1940. Ultimately the craft evolved into the military helicopter, the R-4.

193. What was the first helicopter used by the American military? The first helicopter built for military service in the United States was the Sikorsky XR-4, which was delivered to Wright Field, Ohio in 1942. As a result of successful trials, deliveries of the craft, now known as the YR-4, began to the Army in 1944. A YR-4 was also the first helicopter to be flown from a ship during trials in the Long Island Sound in May 1943.

194. What was the first delivery by air of military airplanes from one country to another? The first delivery by air of military aircraft direct from American to British territory was made on June 21, 1940. A flight of 55 Northrop A-17A attack bombers flew from Mitchel Field, Long Island to Halifax, Nova Scotia, for delivery to England.

195. What American fighter of World War II remained in production the longest? The longest production run of any World War II fighter was the Vought F4U Corsair, which first flew on May 29, 1940. Delivery commenced on October 3, 1942. The last Corsair did not roll off Vought's Dallas production line until December 1952. It was also the last American piston-engined fighter to remain in production. Corsairs were also used during the Korean War as dive bombers.

196. What was the first naval battle in which the combatants relied solely upon airplanes? The first naval battle in which warships relied solely upon airplanes was the Battle of the Coral Sea, fought on May 7–9, 1942, between U.S. Navy Task Force 17 and Vice-Admiral Tokogi's Carrier Striking Force. The battle was fought to prevent a Japanese invasion of Port Moresby and thus enabling air strikes against Australia. Each side lost one aircraft carrier, however the Japanese lost more aircraft and had more ships damaged. Thus it was considered to be an American victory.

197. What was the most aircraft one country ever lost in one day of aerial combat? The worst losses of aircraft by one country in one day, both as a result of aerial combat and anti-aircraft fire, were by the German Luftwaffe on May 10, 1940. On that day Germany invaded France, Belgium, and Holland and were opposed by the air forces of those countries as well as that of Great Britain. According to Luftwaffe records, 304 aircraft were destroyed and 51 damaged. Aircrew casualties amounted to 267 killed, 133 wounded, and 340 missing.

198. Who was the first American pilot to die in action during World War II? The first American pilot to die in action during the Second World War was William Fiske, serving with the Royal Air Force, on August 17, 1940. Fiske fell in action at Tangmere, England during the Battle of Britain.

199. Who was the most successful woman fighter pilot of World War II? The most successful woman fighter pilot of the Second World War was Soviet pilot Lieutenant Lydia Litvak. Serving with the 73rd Fighter Air Regiment, flying Yak fighters, she shot down 12 German aircraft before being killed in action on August 1, 1943 at the age of 22.

200. Who was the first American ace of World War II? The first American ace of World War II was Navy Lieutenant Edward "Butch" O'hare. On February 20, 1942, O'hare, flying a Grumman Wildcat, attacked and shot down five Japanese bombers attempting to attack the aircraft carrier *Lexington.* O'hare won the Congressional Medal of Honor for the exploit.

201. Who was the leading American ace of World War II? The leading American ace of World War II was Major Richard I. Bong, who flew entirely in the Pacific theatre of operations. Bong, who flew Lockheed P-38 Lightnings, had 40 aerial victories at the war's end. He was the first American to surpass Rickenbacker's World War I total, and this is still the most victories by an American aviator. Bong was killed in August 1945, at the age of 25, test flying the Lockheed P-80.

202. What was the only airship shot down during World War II? The only airship shot down during World War II was the U.S. Navy K-74. While attempting to bomb a German submarine surfaced off the coast of Florida, the airship was shot down by a deck gun on the German submarine on July 18, 1943. All but one of the crew were saved.

203. What was the most aircraft ever shot down by an American in one day? The most enemy aircraft ever shot down by an American in one day was nine, a record held by Navy Commander David McCampbell. On October 24, 1944, during the Second Battle of the Philippine Sea, McCampbell, in a Grumman F6F Hellcat, shot down nine Japanese Zeros. He was awarded the Congressional Medal of Honor, personally presented by President Roosevelt at the White House.

204. When did an airplane first fly into a hurricane? The first time an airplane flew directly into a hurricane was on September 14, 1944. Colonel Floyd Wood and Major Harry Wexler, flying a Douglas A-20 Havoc, near Florida, successfully carried out the first attempt to fly into the heart of a hurricane to obtain valuable scientific data.

205. What was the first, and only, enemy aircraft to bomb the continental United States? The only enemy aircraft to ever bomb the continental United States was a Japanese Yokosuka E-14Y Glen. Piloted by warrant officer Noburo Fujita, the E-14Y was catapulted from the submarine I-25 twice in September 1942. On September 9 and 25 it dropped four 165-pound phosphorus bombs in the woods near Brookings, Oregon, in the vain hope of starting huge forest fires.

206. What was the last American military biplane to remain in production? The last American biplanes built for the military, and possible combat use, were the Grumman/Columbia J2F-6 Ducks. Designed for transport, reconnaissance, and air/sea rescue work for the Navy, Ducks were in continuous production between 1934 and 1945. Perhaps the most famous exploit by a Duck was when one discovered a secret German weather base in Greenland in 1944.

207. What was the U.S. Navy's first monoplane fighter? The Navy's first monoplane fighter was the Brewster F2A Buffalo. The F2A first flew in January 1938, but due to poor handling, low speed, and structural problems, only 108 were built before production ended in 1942. Approximately 250 export versions were built for England and Finland. The F2A saw very limited and unsuccessful service with the U.S. Navy in World War II, but they were successfully employed by Finland in their "Winter War" against the Soviet Union.

208. What was the most produced fighter in American history? The most produced fighter in American history was the Republic P-47 Thunderbolt. First flown in May 1941, the P-47 became one of the mainstay fighters for the Army Air Corps during World War II. They were used for fighter sweep, bomber escort, and low-level fighter-bomber missions during the war. Built in factories in Farmingdale, New York and Evansville, Indiana, 15,683 P-47s were built through 1945.

209. What was the greatest distance anyone has ever fallen from an aircraft without a parachute and survived? The greatest distance anyone has ever fallen without a parachute and survived is 22,000 feet. In January 1942, Lieutenant I. M. Chisov of the USSR was thrown from an exploding Ilyushin IL-4. Unconscious, he never opened his parachute, but fortunately he struck the ground on the side of a steep snow-covered ravine and slid to the bottom, gradually slowing his fall. He survived with a fractured pelvis and spinal damage, but continued to serve in the USSR Air Force until 1970.

210. What was the first carrier-based fighter with a tricycle undercarriage? The first operational carrier-based fighter with a tricycle undercarriage was the Grumman F7F Tigercat, which first flew in December 1943. Powered by two Pratt & Whitney R-2800s, and with a top speed of 435 mph, the Tigercat was too late to see service in World War II. However, Marine night-fighter versions did see combat in the Korean War.

211. Who was the first Kamikaze pilot? The first official Kamikaze pilot was Japanese Navy Lieutenant Yukio Seki, who formed the first Kamikaze (suicide) unit in October 1944. The unit was equipped with Mitsubishi Zero-Sen fighters armed with 250-pound bombs. Lieutenant Seki made the first successful Kamikaze attack on October 25, 1944, flying from Mabalacat. He crashed into the American escort carrier *St. Lo,* which sank as a result of the damage inflicted.

212. What was the world's first jet airplane? The first true turbojet airplane was Germany's Heinkel HE-178 which was first flown on August 27, 1939 at Rostock by Captain Erich Warsitz. The then-secret plane was powered by an HE S-3B jet engine designed by Dr. Hans Von Ohain.

213. What was the first flight by an American jet? The first flight by a turbojet aircraft in the United States was on October 2, 1942. On that day a Bell XP-59A with a General Electric I-A engine first flew over Muroc (now Edwards) Air Base, California.

214. What was the first jet aircraft to enter operational service? The first jet fighter to become operational with any air force was the German Messerschmitt ME-262A-1. Powered by two Junkers Jumo 109 engines, the swept-wing fighter was armed with four 30mm cannons as well as underwing rockets and it could reach 500 mph. The ME-262 entered operational service with EK-262 at Lochfeld on June 3, 1944, and the next day one shot down a B-17 "Flying Fortress," marking the first jet "kill."

215. What was the first airplane to have an ejection seat? The first airplane to have an ejection seat was the experimental German HE-280 fighter, which first flew on April 2, 1941. The seat was a compressed-air operated device. The first emergency ejection was made over Rechlin, Germany, on January 13, 1942, when the HE-280 prototype lost control due to heavy icing. The pilot, Major Schenk, ejected at 7800 feet and made a safe landing.

216. What was the first rocket-powered fighter to see combat? The first, and only, rocket-powered plane to see combat was the German Messerschmitt ME-163 Komet. Powered by a Walther HWK 109 liquid-fuel rocket motor, the ME-163 was armed with two 30mm cannons. First flown in 1941, the Komet commenced service in August 1944, and they only destroyed about a dozen allied aircraft in all. The only pilot known to have gained two victories was Oberleutnant August Hochtel. The ME-163 could attain speeds of 600 mph during its six-minute powered boost to Altitude.

217. Who was the most successful fighter pilot in history? The most successful fighter pilot in the world was Germany's Major Erich Hartmann. He first saw combat duty at the age of 20 in October 1942 on the Eastern Front. Flying entirely Messerschmitt BF-109s, Hartmann flew in a cool, calculating manner, preferring to close to a very close range before firing. By September 20, 1943, he scored his 100th kill, all over Soviet aircraft. On March 2, 1944, he scored his 200th victory, and during the summer of 1944 he destroyed 78 aircraft in four weeks. By August 23 he reached 300 victories, the first ever to do so. By the war's end in May 1945, Hartmann had 352 confirmed victories—260 against fighters. Having survived the war, Hartmann spent ten years in a Soviet prison camp. Upon release he rejoined the Luftwaffe and rose to the rank of General.

218. What was the most aircraft of one type ever produced in one month? The most aircraft of one type ever produced in one month was the F6F Hellcat by Grumman in Bethpage, New York. In March 1945, they produced 605 Hellcats, an aircraft production record that has never been equaled.

219. What was the first airplane to drop an atomic bomb? The first airplane to ever drop an atomic bomb was a Boeing B-29 bomber, the *Enola Gay,* piloted by Colonel Paul Tibbets on August 6, 1945. The aircraft, from the 509th Composite Group, released the bomb at 31,000 feet over Hiroshima, Japan. The resulting explosion destroyed five square miles of the city and killed approximately 100,000 people.

The Jet Age

220. What was the largest flying boat ever to fly? The largest flying boat in the world was the Hughes H.2 Hercules. The 190-ton eight-engine aircraft had a wingspan of 320 feet. It was designed to carry 400 troops across the Atlantic nonstop during World War II. After ten years of construction it only flew once, piloted by Howard Hughes. The plane rose 70 feet in the air for about ¾ of a mile in Long Beach Harbor, California on November 2, 1947. The aircraft is now in a museum in Oregon. This was also the largest aircraft ever built.

221. Who was the first person issued a summons for flying a helicopter illegally? The first person issued a summons for flying a helicopter illegally was Roland Roelofs of Riverdale, Maryland, on April 23, 1948. Roelofs was given a violation for buzzing the White House and Capitol Building at an altitude of 200 feet.

222. What was the first airplane to fly around the world nonstop? The first nonstop flight around the world, covering a total of 23,452 miles, was accomplished by an Air Force Boeing B-50 bomber, *Lucky Lady*, between March 2–6, 1949. Piloted by Captain James Gallagher and a crew of 13, the flight required 94 hours and the plane was refueled four times in flight.

223. What is the fastest a woman has ever flown in a piston-engine aircraft? The fastest a woman has ever flown in a piston-engine aircraft is 469 mph. The record was set by Jacqueline Cochran, flying a North American P-51C Mustang on December 10, 1947 at Coachella Valley, California.

224. What was the first landplane commercial flight between the United States and Europe? The first landplane commercial flight between the United States and Europe occurred on October 24, 1945. An American Overseas airlines war surplus Douglas C-54 Skymaster arrived at Hurn Airfield, England, flying from LaGuardia Airport, New York in 14 hours, 5 minutes.

225. Who made the world's first supersonic flight? The first man to fly faster than the speed of sound was Captain Charles Yeager on October

14, 1947. Yeager was flying the experimental rocket-powered Bell X-1 over Muroc (now Edwards), California. The supersonic flight, which reached 960 mph at 70,000 feet, was kept secret, for national security reasons, for several years. The X-1's fuel supply only lasted for ten minutes, so it was released at 30,000 feet by a B-29.

226. What was the first jet aircraft to operate from an aircraft carrier? The world's first jet to operate from an aircraft carrier was a DeHavilland Vampire. It was flown by Lieutenant Commander E. M. Brown from the HMS *Ocean* on December 3, 1945.

227. What was the first American jet to operate from an aircraft carrier? The first American jet to operate from an aircraft carrier was a McDonnell XFD-1 Phantom flown from the USS *Franklin D. Roosevelt,* as she lay off Cape Henry, Virginia on July 21, 1946. The aircraft was piloted by Lieutenant Commander James Davidson. The takeoff run was 460 feet.

228. What was the first airliner to be hijacked? The first airliner to be hijacked was a Cathay Pacific Catalina Flying Boat. On June 16, 1948, at Macao, the aircraft was seized by a gang of Chinese bandits seeking ransom for the passengers. The pilot resisted and was shot, the plane crashed, killing all on board except for one of the bandits.

229. What was the first department store to sell airplanes? The first department store to sell airplanes was Wanamaker's in New York City. On October 5, 1945, they placed three models of Piper aircraft on display.

230. What was the first baseball team to travel entirely by air? The first major league team to use air transportation for its full schedule was the New York Yankees. On April 9, 1946, they signed a contract with United Air Lines to travel by air throughout the 1946 season.

231. What was the fastest four-engine propeller-driven aircraft? The world's fastest four-engine propeller-driven aircraft was the Republic XF-12 Rainbow. Designed for the Air Force as a high-altitude strategic reconnaissance aircraft, the XF-12 first flew on February 4, 1946. Powered by four Pratt & Whitney R-4360 engines, the highly streamlined aircraft obtained the speed of 440 mph in May 1946. After the Air Force cancelled the program in 1947, unsuccessful attempts were made to sell the aircraft as a high-speed civil airliner, but the glut of cheap post-war military aircraft precluded this. Only two were built.

232. What was the only American fighter with a rocket engine? The only American fighter equipped with a rocket engine was the Republic

XF-91 Thunderceptor. The aircraft's primary propulsion was a GE J47 jet engine, but it was also equipped with a Reaction Motors XLR-11 rocket engine in order to give it a very short rate of climb to altitude and a limited supersonic ability. Two XF-91s were built, and they were successfully flown many times between 1949 and 1953 on both jet and rocket power, however no further production orders were placed due to advances in jet engine technology. Top speed was 984 mph.

233. What was the first American use of an ejection seat? The first emergency use in the United States of an ejection seat occurred on August 9, 1949. On that day Lt. J.L. Fruin of the U.S. Navy made an emergency ejection from his McDonnell F2H-1 Banshee at a speed of 575 mph near Waterboro, South Carolina.

234. What was the first solo transatlantic flight in a jet? The first solo transatlantic flight in a jet was made by Colonel David Schilling on September 22, 1950. The flight was from Manston, England to Limestone, Maine—3300 miles in 10 hours, 1 minute. The flight was made in a Republic F-84E Thunderjet that was aerial refueled three times enroute.

235. When did a guided missile first destroy an airplane in flight? The first time a guided missile intercepted an aircraft in flight was November 4, 1951. On that day a developmental American Nike-Ajax surface-to-air missile tracked and destroyed a B-17 drone, at 19,000 feet, over the White Sands Proving Ground, New Mexico.

236. What was the fastest turboprop airplane? The fastest turboprop airplane ever was the Republic XF-84H. Designed as a naval carrier fighter with jet-type performance, only two XF-84Hs were built. The XF-84H's 12-foot propeller was driven by an Allison XT-40 engine, allowing the plane to reach the speed of 665 mph in September 1955. Still the fastest propeller-driven aircraft to date, the XF-84H was rendered obsolete by advances in jet aircraft and aircraft carrier technology.

237. What was the world's first supersonic bomber? The world's first supersonic bomber was the Convair B-58 Hustler, which first flew on November 11, 1956. The Hustler was unique on many counts. It carried its offensive weapons in a jettisonable pod under its belly. Defensive weapons were limited to a remotely controlled multi-barrel Gatling gun in the tail. The airframe of each aircraft cost more than its weight in gold. During flight trials, B-58s attained speeds of up to Mach 2.09, and flew continuously at supersonic speed for up to 1½ hours.

238. What is the longest recorded parachute descent? The longest recorded parachute descent was made by Lt. Colonel William Rankin of the U.S. Marine Corps on July 26, 1959. Ejecting from his Vought F8U Crusader at 47,000 feet, Rankin descended through a violent thunderstorm over North Carolina. Strong vertical air currents in the storm repeatedly forced him upwards so that it took him 48 minutes to reach the ground.

239. What was the first U.S. Navy jet to see combat? The first U.S. Navy jet to engage in aerial combat was a Grumman F9F-2 Panther from the USS *Valley Forge* off Korea on July 3, 1950, against North Korean forces. On November 9, 1950, a Navy pilot in an F9F shot down a Mig-15, thus becoming the first U.S. Navy jet pilot to shoot down another jet.

240. What was the U.S. Navy's first supersonic aircraft? The first operational supersonic U.S. Navy fighter was the Grumman F11F-1 Tiger. First flown on July 7, 1954, it was powered by a Wright J-67 and carried an armament of four 20mm cannons. Top speed was 890 mph.

241. What is the smallest airplane ever to fly? The smallest man-carrying aircraft ever to fly was the *Bumble Bee Two,* built by Robert Starr of Arizona. It had a wingspan of 5'6" and could reach speeds of up to 190 mph. In 1988 it crashed and was totally destroyed.

242. What was the first American commercial transatlantic jet flight? The first commercial American transatlantic jet flight was made on September 8, 1958. A Pan American Boeing 707 Jet Clipper America departed Idlewild (Kennedy) Airport, New York, and landed in London, 7 hours, 28 minutes later.

243. Who was the first woman to fly faster than the speed of sound? The first woman to fly faster than the speed of sound was the American Jacqueline Cochran, flying a North American F-86 Sabre on May 18, 1953. On that flight she also established a new world speed record for women of 652 mph.

244. Who was the first person to make a solo flight over the North Pole? The first person to fly alone over the North Pole was Captain Charles Blair of Port Washington, New York, on May 30, 1951. Blair flew the pole from Fairbanks, Alaska to Idlewild (Kennedy) Airport, New York—3450 miles—in a modified North American P-51 Mustang, the *Excaliber III,* in 9 hours, 31 minutes.

245. What was the first commercial jet aircraft? The first jet airliner to enter commercial service was the British deHavilland DH-106 Comet. Its first commercial flight was on May 2, 1952, when a British Overseas Airways DH-106 flew between London and Johannesburg, South Africa. It carried 36 passengers and flew the 6724 miles in 23 hours, 34 minutes (with five refueling stops).

246. What was the first jet airliner crash? The first jet airliner crash occurred on March 3, 1953, when a Canadian Pacific DeHavilland Comet crashed on takeoff in Karachi, Pakistan. All eleven on board were killed. The accident was said to have been caused by the pilot lifting the plane's nose too high on takeoff, causing it to stall.

247. When did a jet fighter first shoot down another jet? The first aerial victory to be gained by the pilot of one jet aircraft over another was achieved on November 8, 1950, during the Korean War. Lieutenant Russell Brown of the 51st Fighter Interceptor Wing, flying a Lockheed F-80 Shooting Star, shot down a Chinese Mig-15 over the Yalu River, the border between North Korea and China.

248. When did transcontinental jet passenger service first begin? Transcontinental jet passenger service first began on January 25, 1959, when an American Airlines Boeing 707 made the trip between Los Angeles, California, and Idlewild (Kennedy) Airport, New York, with 112 passengers, in 4 hours, 3 minutes. The plane was piloted by Captain Charles Macatee of Huntington, New York. Later that same day a flight from New York to Los Angeles was made in 6 hours 33 minutes.

249. When was the first time Americans travelled more by air than by trains? The first time in U.S. history that air-passenger miles exceeded rail-passenger miles was during 1952. For that year air miles totalled 10,679,281,000, while rail miles totalled 10,224,718,000. During 1953, for the first time, aircraft became the prime mover for U.S. travellers going over 200 miles.

250. What was the first American town to attempt to regulate air traffic at a major airport? The first American town to attempt to regulate air traffic at a major airport was Cedarhurst, Long Island, New York. In 1952, the Village of Cedarhurst issued an ordinance restricting low-altitude approaches to nearby Idlewild (Kennedy) Airport. On December 13, 1956, the U.S. Court of Appeals upheld an injunction voiding the ordinance. The Court held that the ordinance was in conflict with the paramount federal authority to regulate flight altitudes. The ruling stands to this day.

251. What is the greatest altitude anyone has ever made a parachute jump from? The highest parachute jump, and the longest free fall, was made by Captain Joseph Kittinger of the U.S. Air Force, over Tularosa, New Mexico on August 19, 1960. Kittinger jumped out of a balloon gondola at 102,000 feet and free fell 84,700 feet in 4 minutes, 38 seconds. During this fall he reached a speed of 614 mph in the high thin air. His parachute deployed at 17,500 feet and he landed after a total time of 13 minutes, 45 seconds.

252. What is the fastest commercial flight between Los Angeles and New York? The fastest commercial airline flight between Los Angeles and New York is 3 hours, 38 minutes. The flight was made by an American Airlines Boeing 707-123, under Captain Wylie Drummond, at a speed of 680 mph, between Los Angeles and Idlewild (Kennedy) Airport, New York on April 10, 1963. There was an unusually strong tailwind in the jetstream that day.

253. What was the heaviest load ever lifted by a single-engine airplane? The heaviest load ever lifted by a single-engine airplane was 14,500 pounds by a Republic F-105D Thunderchief. The F-105 was originally designed as a long-range nuclear bomber, but during the Vietnam War it was pressed into service as a tactical bomber. On October 7, 1961, during a special test at Eglin Air Force Base, Florida, an F-105 dropped 14,500 pounds of bombs to demonstrate its ability to deliver conventional ordnance.

254. What was the fastest airplane in the world? The fastest airplane in the world was the North American X-15A-2 research aircraft. Three X-15s were built in the late 1950s and one was upgraded to the X-15A-2. Air launched from a B-52 bomber, the greatest altitude reached was 354,200 feet (67 miles) by J. A. Walker on August 22, 1963. The highest speed reached was 4534 mph (Mach 6.72) by W. J. Knight on October 3, 1967. Power for the X-15 was a Thiokol XLR-99-RM-2 liquid fuel rocket engine with a 57,000 pound thrust.

255. What was the first solo around-the-world flight by a woman? The first woman to make a solo around-the-world flight was Shiela Scott of England. Between May 18 and June 20, 1966, she made the 29,000 mile flight in her Piper Comanche *Myth Too.*

256. What was the first nonstop transatlantic flight by a helicopter? The first nonstop New York-to-Paris flight by a helicopter took place between May 31 and June 1, 1967. Two Sikorsky HH-3Es made the flight in 30 hours, 46 minutes, each being aerially refueled nine times enroute.

257. What was the first "wide body" jet airliner? The first wide-body jet was the Boeing 747 Jumbo Jet, which first flew on February 9, 1969. The flight was from Paine Field, Washington, and the pilot was Jack Waddell. The new wide-bodied airliner was capable of carrying 360 passengers, thus becoming the largest commercial airliner until that time. Boeing 747s first entered service with Pan American Airways in January 1970.

258. What was America's first variable-geometry fighter? America's first "swing wing" fighter, in which the wings can move forward and back in order to achieve various flight conditions, was the Grumman F-14A Tomcat. The U.S. Navy fighter first flew on December 21, 1970, and it remained in production through 1993. Many are still in service with the Navy.

259. When was the first, and only, transatlantic speed race for aircraft? The one and only transatlantic air race was sponsored by the English newspaper *The Daily Mail* in May 1969, for the fastest journey between the top of the Empire State Building in New York and the top of the Post Office Tower in London. The 5000-pound prize was won by Royal Navy Lieutenants Brian Davies and Peter Goddard, flying a McDonnell Douglas F-4K Phantom II. Total time was 5 hours, 11 minutes, with a flying time of 4 hours, 36 minutes.

260. What was the first nuclear-powered aircraft carrier? The first nuclear-powered aircraft carrier was the USS *Enterprise,* launched at Newport News, Virginia on September 24, 1960. Fitted with eight water-cooled nuclear reactors, she was also the largest warship ever built at 1101 feet long. The *Enterprise* was also the most expensive warship built until then, with a cost of $445 million. She carries 440 officers, 4160 enlisted men, and 100 aircraft.

261. What is the highest a manned balloon has ever flown? The world altitude record for balloons is held by Commander Malcolm Ross, U.S. Navy. On May 4, 1961, he rose to an altitude of 113,739 feet over the Gulf of Mexico in a special research balloon.

262. Who was the first man to eject from an aircraft at supersonic speed? The first man to eject from an aircraft at supersonic speed was George F. Smith, a test pilot for North American Aviation, who ejected from an F-100 Super Sabre on February 26, 1955, off Laguna Beach, California. After failure of the flight controls, and in a dive, Smith ejected at Mach 1.05 (720 mph). Smith spent five days in a coma, after which he eventually recovered from his various head, eye, leg, and intestinal injuries, and ultimately resumed his test pilot duties.

263. What is the first company in the world to produce 100,000 aircraft? The first company in the world to produce 100,000 aircraft is the Cessna Aircraft Corporation of Wichita, Kansas. They reached this figure on May 26, 1972.

264. What was the world's first supersonic transport (SST)? The world's first SST was the Tupolev TU-144, which was first flown by the Soviet Union on December 31, 1968. Largely the same as the Aerospatiale-British Aerospace Corporation Concorde, the TU-144 was developed in secrecy. Only twelve TU-144s were built and they only saw limited freight service between Moscow and Alma Ata in 1977–78. Meanwhile, the Concorde, first flown in March, 1969, remained in regular service until August 2000.

265. What was the first supersonic transport to begin passenger service? The world's first passenger services by a supersonic airliner began on January 21, 1976. On that day British Airways and Air France Concordes took off simultaneously for Bahrain and Rio de Janeiro.

266. What is the fastest transatlantic flight to date? The fastest flight between New York and London was made by a Lockheed SR-71 Blackbird on July 1, 1974. Flown by Major James Sullivan USAF, the flight took 1 hour, 54 minutes at a speed of 1807 mph.

267. What is the highest a piston-engine amphibian has ever flown? The altitude record for piston-engine amphibians is 32,883 feet. The record was set on July 4, 1973, by Lieutenant Charles Manning, USAF, flying a Grumman HU-16B Albatross over Homestead, Florida.

268. What is the highest a helicopter has ever flown? The highest a helicopter has ever flown is 40,820 feet. The record was set by Jean Boulet of France, flying an Alouette SA 315 Lama on June 21, 1972 over Istres, France.

269. What is the fastest a jet plane has ever flown? The fastest jet plane in the world is the twin engine Lockheed SR-71A Blackbird, originally designed for strategic reconnaissance. On July 28, 1976, one was clocked at 2193 mph over Beale Air Force Base, California. The pilot on that day was Captain Eldon Joersz, USAF.

270. Who made the first transatlantic balloon flight? The first transatlantic balloon flight was made by the *Double Eagle II* between August

11 and 17, 1978. With a crew of Ben Abruzzo, Maxie Anderson, and Larry Newman, the helium balloon departed Presque Isle, Maine and landed at Miserey, France 137 hours, 6 minutes later. They were the 14th crew to attempt a transatlantic balloon flight.

271. What was the world's worst airline crash? The world's worst airline crash occurred on March 27, 1977 at Tenerife Airport in the Canary Islands. During bad weather, KLM and Pan American Boeing 747s collided on the runway killing 581 people. The worst airline crash in the United States occurred on May 25, 1979 at O'Hare Airport, Chicago. On takeoff, an American Airlines DC-10 had an engine fall off causing it to crash, killing 275 people.

272. What is the highest a jet plane has ever flown? The highest a jet plane has ever flown is 123,523 feet. The record was set by Alexander Fedotov of the Soviet Union on August 31, 1977. Fedotov was flying a modified Mig 25 Foxbat over Podmoscovnoe, USSR.

273. Who made the first man-powered flight across the English Channel? The first man-powered flight across the English Channel was made by Bryan Allen on June 12, 1979. Allen was flying (pedalling) the 75-pound, 94-foot wingspan *Gossamer Albatross*. The flight was from Dover to Cape Gris Nez, France—21 miles flown in 2 hours, 49 minutes.

274. What was the longest anyone has ever stayed aloft in a hang glider? The longest anyone has ever stayed aloft in a hang glider is 34 hours, 3 minutes. The record was set by James Will in a Gemini 165 over Makapuu Point, Hawaii on June 3–4, 1986.

275. What was the first transpacific balloon flight? Between November 9 and 12, 1981, Ben Abruzzo, Larry Newman, Ron Clark, and Rocky Aoki travelled between Nagashima, Japan and Cavello, California non-stop in an experimental Raven balloon—a distance of 5208 miles.

276. What was the first, and only, airplane to fly around the world nonstop and nonrefueled? The only nonstop, nonrefueled, around-the-world flight was made by Dick Rutan and Jeana Yeager in the Rutan-designed *Voyager* between December 14 and 23, 1986. The twin engine aircraft departed and returned to Edwards Air Force Base, California. The flight took 216 hours, 3 minutes at an average speed of 115 mph. Total distance covered was 24,986 miles.

277. What is the fastest a piston-engine aircraft has ever flown? The fastest a piston-engine aircraft has ever flown is 528 mph. The record was set on August 21, 1989, by Lyle Shelton in a modified Grumman F8F Bearcat, *Rare Bear,* equipped with a 3800-hp Wright 3350 engine.

278. What is the only major airline that has never had a fatal accident? The only major airline that has never had a fatal accident is Qantas of Australia. Founded in 1920 as the Queensland and Northwest Territories Aerial Service, Qantas began service with one war-surplus Armstrong Whitworth FK-8 able to carry two passengers in an open cockpit. Qantas was founded with the belief that money could be made flying passengers over the hostile Australian outback. It has since expanded into a worldwide operation using over 100 jet airliners.

279. Who holds the world record for consecutive loops in an aircraft? The current world record for consecutive inside loops in an aircraft is 2368, set by David Childs. Childs was flying a Bellanca Decathlon over North Pole, Arkansas on August 9, 1986.

280. What is the farthest anyone has ever flown in a man-powered aircraft? The farthest anyone has ever flown in a man-powered aircraft is 71½ miles between Crete and Santorini Island, Greece. The flight took 3 hours, 54 minutes and was made by Kanellos Kanellopoules in the *Daedalus* on April 23, 1988.

281. What is the highest a glider has ever flown? The highest a glider has ever flown is 49,009 feet. The record was set by Robert Harris flying a Grob G-102 over California City, California on February 17, 1986.

282. What is the fastest coast-to-coast flight in a jet aircraft? The fastest flight between Los Angeles and Washington, D.C., was made by a Lockheed SR-71A Blackbird on March 6, 1990. Flown by Lieutenant Colonels Ed Yielding and J. T. Vida, the flight took 1 hour, 8 minutes and was flown at a speed of 2144 mph. This was the only time a sonic boom has travelled uninterrupted from coast to coast.

283. What is the world's heaviest airplane? The world's heaviest airplane is the Russian Antonov AN-225 Mriya (Dream). The six-engine cargo jet weighs 660 tons, and in March 1989 lifted 345,000 pounds for a new world record.

284. What is the most people ever carried by an airplane? The most people ever carried on an airplane was 1088 on an El Al Boeing 747 on May 24, 1991. The passengers were Ethiopian Jewish refugees, fleeing Ethiopia to Israel as part of "Operation Solomon."

285. What was the first circumnavigation of the Earth by balloon? The first around-the-world balloon flight was made by Bertrand Piccard and Brian Jones in the Breitling *Orbiter 3* between March 1 and 20, 1999. They departed from Switzerland, travelling eastward, and eventually circled the world and landed in central Africa.

286. What was the highest anyone has ever flown in a powered parachute? On April 27, 2000, Bud Gish flew a parachute powered by a 50-hp Rotax engine to a new world record of 17,054 feet. The flight was made near Anchorage, Alaska, and Gish experienced extreme temperatures to 20 degrees below zero.

Rockets and Spaceflight

287. When were rockets first used in warfare? In the year 1280, the Syrian military historian Al-Hasan Al-Rammah wrote the book, *Of Fighting on Horseback and with War Engines.* The book gave instructions for producing rockets which he describes as "Chinese Arrows," so they were certainly in use by this time. The Chinese appear to have used rockets as early as 1232 when they repelled Mongols besieging the town of Kai-Fung-Fu.

288. When were rockets first used in warfare by a western army? In 1805, Colonel William Congreve of England developed large solid-fuel rockets at the Woolwich Arsenal. The 32-pound rockets could travel approximately one mile and deliver an explosive charge. By 1806, a Rocket Corps became part of the British Army, and rockets were also fired from ships since they had no recoil. The British first used them on October 8, 1806, during the Napoleonic Wars, when 18 rocket boats attacked Boulogne Harbor. Many of the rockets overshot the French fleet, setting fire to parts of the town. They were also extensively used during the September 1814 attack on Baltimore's Fort McHenry.

289. When was the world's first liquid-propellant rocket flight? The world's first successful liquid-propellant rocket was built by Dr. Robert Goddard of Worcester, Massachusetts. On March 16, 1926, his nine-foot tall rocket flew briefly at Auburn, Massachusetts. The rocket consisted of a tubular steel frame with the engine at the top and the shielded liquid oxygen and gasoline tanks beneath it.

290. When was a rocket first used for scientific purposes? A rocket was first used for scientific research purposes on July 17, 1929. On that day Dr. Robert Goddard launched a barometer, thermometer, and camera in one of his liquid fuel rockets. The instruments were recovered by parachute.

291. Who was the first person killed by a liquid-fuel rocket? The first person killed by the explosion of a liquid-fuel rocket was Max Valier of Germany on May 17, 1930. Valier was fueling a steel-cased rocket motor with kerosene and liquid oxygen when it exploded in his workshop near Berlin. The rocket was to be used on his rocket-car, *Rak-7.*

292. What was the world's first gyroscopically-controlled rocket? The world's first gyroscopically-controlled rocket was an 11-foot-long liquid-fuel rocket launched by Dr. Robert Goddard at Roswell, New Mexico on April 19, 1932. The on-board gyroscope controlled vanes that deflected the rocket's exhaust in order to steer it. The rocket reached an altitude of 135 feet on its first flight.

293. When was the first time airmail was sent by rocket? The first rocket airmail flight was made on February 23, 1936, at Greenwood Lake, New York. The flight was made in an 11-foot long liquid-fuel rocket, named the *Gloria,* built by Willy Ley. The flight carried 4323 letters and 1826 postcards and lasted about 45 seconds.

294. What was the world's first liquid-fuel propelled rocket-plane? The world's first liquid-fuel rocket-propelled aircraft was the German Heinkel HE-176, which first flew at Peenemunde on June 20, 1939. Flown by Erich Warsitz, the plane was powered by a Walther rocket engine of 1100 pounds thrust. The plane had a pressurized cockpit that could be separated from the fuselage and recovered by parachute.

295. What was the world's first ballistic missile used in war? The first military long-range ballistic missile was the 46-foot long German V-2, first test flown at Peenemunde on October 3, 1942. On September 8, 1944, V-2s, with one-ton warheads, were first launched against London in retaliation for Allied air attacks on Germany. Eventually 4320 V-2s were launched, 1120 against London, and they killed 2511 people and injured nearly 6000. V-2s were built by slave labor in an underground assembly plant in the Harz Mountains.

296. What was the first liquid-fuel two-stage missile? The first liquid-fuel two-stage missile was a "Bumper," launched from White Sands Proving Ground, New Mexico on February 24, 1949. The missile consisted of a Wac Corporal rocket mounted atop a German V-2.

297. What was the world's first artificial satellite? The world's first artificial satellite was *Sputnik,* launched by the Soviet Union on October 4, 1957. The 24"-diameter, 184-pound spacecraft was launched atop an R.7 ICBM from the Baikonur Cosmodrome. *Sputnik,* meaning traveller in Russian, provided basic information on the density and temperature of the upper atmosphere, as well as on orbital decay. Its launch proved shocking and disturbing to many in the west, and it began the "space race" that culminated with the Apollo 11 Moon landing.

298. What was the first animal launched into space? The first animal launched into space was a female dog named Laika, by the Soviet Union, in *Sputnik 2,* on November 3, 1957. The intent was to transmit basic information on the biological effect of spaceflight. There was no provision for recovery and the dog died when the air supply ran out.

299. What was the first American artificial satellite? The first American artificial satellite was *Explorer 1,* launched by a Juno rocket from Cape Canaveral, Florida, on January 31, 1958. The Juno was developed by Dr. Werner Von Braun and an Army team at the Redstone arsenal in Alabama. Instrumented by Dr. James Van Allen, *Explorer's* major discovery was that Earth was girdled by radiation belts.

300. What was the first man-made object to go to the Moon? The first man-made object to impact the Moon was the Soviet *Lunik 2* on September 12, 1959. On October 4, 1959 the Soviets launched *Lunik 3* which became the first spacecraft to circumnavigate the Moon and photograph its far side.

301. When was the first time missiles were launched from a submerged submarine? The first time missiles were launched from a submerged submarine was on July 20, 1960. Two Polaris missiles were launched from the USS *George Washington,* 25 miles east of Cape Canaveral.

302. What was the first meteorological satellite? The first meteorological satellite was *Tiros 1,* launched by the United States on April 1, 1960. The drum-shaped spacecraft was 22 inches in diameter and weighed 283 pounds. Launched atop a Thor-Able rocket from Cape Canaveral, it took photographs of Earth's cloud cover from an altitude of 450 miles.

303. What was the first communications satellite? The first experimental communications satellite was *Echo 1,* launched by the United States on August 12, 1960. The satellite was a silver mylar balloon that inflated to 100 feet in diameter in space. It was successfully used to reflect radio waves from ground-based transmitters to receiving stations on Earth separated by thousands of miles.

304. What were the first living creatures recovered from Space? The first living creatures recovered from space were two dogs, Belka and Strelka, launched by the Soviet Union on August 19, 1960. The *Sputnik 5* orbital flight was made in a Vostok spacecraft prototype launched on an A-1 rocket. The flight lasted a little over a day. This flight paved the way for manned spaceflight.

305. Who was the first person launched into space? The first human being launched into space was Lieutenant Yuri Gagarin of the Soviet Union on April 12, 1961. In the spacecraft, *Vostok 1,* (meaning east) Gagarin made one orbit of Earth in a flight lasting one hour, 48 minutes. Orbital altitude was between 113 and 204 miles. He was launched on an A-1 rocket from Baikonur, and he was landed via parachute near Smelovoka.

306. Who was the first American launched into space? The first American launched into space was Navy Commander Alan Shepard on May 5, 1961. In the Mercury spacecraft *Freedom 7,* launched from Cape Canaveral on a Redstone rocket, Shepard made a sub-orbital flight to an altitude of 116 miles. The flight lasted 15 minutes and Shepard demonstrated the ability to achieve manual control of the spacecraft under weightlessness.

307. Who was the first person to spend a day in space? The first person to spend a day in space was Major Gherman Titov of the Soviet Union on August 6–7, 1961. Titov, in *Vostok 2,* completed 17 orbits of Earth in 25 hours, 18 minutes.

308. Who was the first American to orbit the Earth? The first American to orbit Earth was Lieutenant Colonel John Glenn on February 20, 1962. In the Mercury 6 spacecraft *Friendship 7,* Glenn completed three orbits of Earth in 4 hours, 55 minutes. He was launched on an Atlas rocket from Cape Canaveral and was recovered near Puerto Rico.

309. What was the first interplanetary space flight? The first interplanetary spacecraft was *Mariner 2,* launched by the United States on August 27, 1962. It travelled 180 million miles and flew within 21,594 miles of Venus on December 14, 1962. *Mariner's* most significant discovery was that Venus has a surface temperature of 800 degrees. The first spacecraft to actually land on another planet was the Soviet Union's *Venus 3,* which was launched on November 16, 1965, and made a hard landing on Venus on March 1, 1966.

310. Who was the first woman in space? The first woman in space was Junior Lieutenant Valentine Tereshkova, age 26, of the Soviet Union on June 16–19, 1963. In the *Vostok 6* spacecraft she completed 48 orbits of Earth in 70 hours, 50 minutes.

311. What was the first three-man spacecraft? The first three-man spacecraft was *Voskhod 1* of the Soviet Union, launched on October 12,

1964. The spacecraft carried Vladimir Kamarov, Konstantin Feoktistov, and Boris Yegarov on a 16-orbit flight lasting 24 hours, 17 minutes. Feoktistov was the spacecraft's designer and Yegarov a doctor, both specialists gaining first-hand experience in spaceflight.

312. Who was the first person to "walk" in space? The first person to make an Extra-Vehicular Activity, or spacewalk, was Lieutenant Colonel Alexei Leonov of the Soviet Union on March 18, 1965. In the *Voskhod 2* spacecraft, along with Pavel Belyayev, the two made a 17-orbit mission in 26 hours, 2 minutes. Leonov's spacewalk lasted approximately 15 minutes.

313. Who was the first American to walk in space? The first American to walk in space was Captain Edward White on June 24, 1965. Along with Captain James McDivitt in the *Gemini 4* spacecraft, the 62-orbit mission lasted 97 hours, 56 minutes. White's spacewalk lasted 21 minutes and he was the first to maneuver in space with a gas-gun.

314. What was the first spacecraft to successfully land on the Moon? The first spacecraft (unmanned) to make a successful soft landing on the Moon was the Soviet Union's *Luna 9*. On January 31, 1966, it landed on the Moon and transmitted panoramic still photos of the terrain.

315. What was the first spacecraft to dock with another in space? The first docking between spacecraft occurred on the *Gemini 8* mission, launched on March 16, 1966. Neil Armstrong and David Scott docked their spacecraft with an unmanned Agena vehicle in Earth orbit. The 6-orbit mission lasted 10 hours, 41 minutes. The flight ended prematurely when a thruster in the *Gemini* malfunctioned causing the combined spacecraft to spin. After separating the spacecraft the astronauts made a safe return to Earth.

316. Who was the first person to die in space? Although no one has actually died in space to date, several people have died on the way up or the way down. The first to do so was Colonel Vladimir Kamarov, of the Soviet Union, on April 24, 1967. Kamarov was making the first manned test in the new *Soyuz* spacecraft. He was killed when the parachute lines of the re-entry module became tangled after returning from orbit, thus prohibiting the parachute from opening properly.

317. What was the first space telescope? The first large-scale space telescope was the Orbiting Astronomical Observatory (OAO), launched on December 7, 1968. Built by Grumman, the 20-foot long space telescope investigated space in the ultraviolet region of the spectrum, outside the distorting influences of Earth's atmosphere.

318. What was the first manned spacecraft to orbit the Moon? The first manned spacecraft to orbit the Moon was *Apollo 8,* launched on December 21, 1968. Commanded by Frank Borman, along with James Lovell and William Anders, *Apollo 8* orbited the Moon ten times in 20 hours, 6 minutes. Total flight time was 147 hours.

319. Who was the first person to walk on the Moon? The first person to set foot on the Moon was Neil A. Armstrong, on July 20, 1969. Commander of the *Apollo 11* mission, Armstrong, along with Edwin "Buzz" Aldrin and Michael Collins, fulfilled President Kennedy's 1961 goal of landing a man on the Moon within the decade. Armstrong and Aldrin, in the Grumman Lunar Module *Eagle,* landed on the Moon's "Sea of Tranquillity" at 4:17 p.m. EST. Armstrong first set foot on the Moon at 8:56 p.m., and, along with Aldrin, made a moonwalk lasting two hours, 31 minutes. Total stay on the Moon was 21 hours, 36 minutes and total mission time was 195 hours, 18 minutes.

320. What was the fastest human beings have ever travelled? The fastest human beings have ever travelled is 24,791 mph. During the *Apollo 10* mission on May 26, 1969, Thomas Stafford, Gene Cernan, and John Young travelled this speed at 76 miles altitude as their Command Module was re-entering Earth's atmosphere.

321. What was the first remote-control vehicle to operate on the Moon? The first remotely-operated vehicle to drive on the Moon was the Soviet Union's *Lunokhod 1,* launched on the *Luna 17* mission on November 10, 1970. The 8-wheeled vehicle was soft-landed on the Moon and steered via a TV/radio link from a control station in the USSR. The vehicle travelled a total distance of almost 6 miles, and sent back more than 200 panoramic pictures.

322. Who was the first person to hit a golf ball on the Moon? The first, and only, person to hit a golf ball on the Moon was Alan Shepard on *Apollo 14* on February 4, 1971. Shepard, an avid golfer, smuggled a golf driver head on board the spacecraft. He then modified the head to fit a rock hammer's extension shaft. As part of a televised demonstration, Shepard took two swings at a golf ball, missing it the first time and driving it on the second swing "for miles and miles."

323. What was the world's first space station? The world's first space station was *Salyut 1,* which was launched by the Soviet Union on April 19,

1971. The 50-foot long, 14-foot diameter space station was first visited by cosmonauts on April 24, 1971.

324. What was the first manned vehicle to drive on the Moon? The first manned vehicle to drive on the Moon was the Boeing Lunar Rover first used on the *Apollo 15* mission. The *Apollo 15* mission, July 26–August 7, 1971, featured a new version of the Lunar Module that could carry more and stay longer on the Moon. The Lunar Rover was carried on the Lunar Module's Descent Stage and was deployed by the astronauts. It was a 4-wheel drive, electrically-powered vehicle capable of speeds up to 15 mph.

325. Who was the last man to walk on the moon? The last man to walk on the moon was Gene Cernan, commander of the Apollo 17 mission on December 13, 1972.

326. What was the first international space mission? The first international space mission was *Apollo-Soyuz* between July 15–24, 1975. The mission involved two Soviets in a Soyuz and three Americans in an Apollo spacecraft. The two spacecraft docked in Earth orbit and remained docked for two days performing experiments.

327 What was the first weather station on Mars? The first weather station on Mars was the *Viking 1* spacecraft, launched by the United States on August 20, 1976. The spacecraft landed softly on Mars' Chryse Planitia on July 20, 1976, and immediately began transmitting photographs, scientific information, and weather data back to Earth. It remained in operation for three years.

328. What was the world's first reusable spacecraft? The world's first reusable spacecraft were the space shuttles, built by the United States in the late 1970s and early 1980s. The spacecraft consisted of a 123-foot long winged orbiter, which could carry up to eight people; an external fuel tank; and two solid rocket boosters used during the launch phase. The first space shuttle, the *Columbia,* flew on April 12–14, 1981 (STS-1), and was crewed by John Young and Robert Crippen. The 36-orbit flight lasted 54 hours. Space shuttles (there are now four) are generally launched monthly in missions lasting up to two weeks. STS-1 was also the first use of solid-fuel rockets in manned spaceflight and the first time a spacecraft landed on a runway.

329. What was the first time a spacecraft was reused? The first manned spacecraft to be reused was the *Columbia* on STS-2 on November 12, 1981, when the *Columbia* was launched again on a 36-orbit mission.

Flown by Joe Engle and Richard Truly, the crew tested the Remote Manipulator System robot arm and carried an Earth Resources Pallet into orbit. This was the first time any craft had returned to space.

330. Who was the first American woman in space? The first American woman in space was Dr. Sally Ride, who was launched on STS-7 on June 18, 1983. This was *Challenger*'s second flight and was crewed by five people.

331. Who was the first astronaut to fly freely in space? The first astronaut to fly freely in space, not attached to a spacecraft in any way, was Bruce McCandless in the Manned Maneuvering Unit (MMU) on February 4, 1984. McCandless, launched on *Challenger STS-41B*, flew freely of the spacecraft with his own maneuverable backpack. The MMU contained its own life support and jet maneuvering system. McCandless thus also became the first human satellite.

332. When was the first time a satellite was repaired in space? The world's first satellite repair in space occurred on STS-41C, the *Challenger* flight launched on April 6, 1984. On that mission Terry Hart and George Nelson spent 7 hours, 18 minutes spacewalking in order to successfully repair the failed *Solar Maximum* spacecraft. The Shuttle rendezvoused with the Solar Max satellite in orbit so the astronauts could perform the repairs in the space shuttle's cargo bay.

333. When was the first time satellites were captured in space and returned to Earth? The first ever satellite retrieval mission was STS-51A, the *Discovery* flight launched on November 8, 1984. On that flight two satellites in uselessly low orbits, *Palapa B-2* and *Westar 6,* were captured by the shuttle and returned to Earth for later successful launches.

334. Who was the oldest person ever in space? The oldest human to fly into space was former Mercury astronaut John Glenn. At age 77, he flew on the space shuttle *Discovery* between October 29 and November 7, 1998.

335. Who was the first woman to command a space shuttle mission? The first woman to command a space shuttle mission was Eileen Collins of Elmira, New York. She commanded STS 93 *Columbia,* which flew from July 23 to 27, 1999.

336. What is the world's first international space station? The world's first international space station (known as ISS), was launched over the course of 12 space shuttle flights beginning in 1998. The space station's components are being built by the United States, Russia, Japan, Canada, and several European countries. It will be assembled over a five-year period with the elements launched on flights by the United States and Russia. The 886,000 pound station will consist of seven pressurized modules, and 6 people at a time will live there. It is expected to become fully operational in 2001.